Anne Robinson
Karen Saxby

FUN
for
Flyers

Student's Book

••• Second edition

CAMBRIDGE
UNIVERSITY PRESS

CAMBRIDGE
UNIVERSITY PRESS

University Printing House, Cambridge CB2 8BS, United Kingdom

Cambridge University Press is part of the University of Cambridge.

It furthers the University's mission by disseminating knowledge in the pursuit of education, learning and research at the highest international levels of excellence.

www.cambridge.org
Information on this title: www.cambridge.org/9780521748568

First published 2006
Second edition published 2010
12th printing 2013

Printed in Italy by L.E.G.O. S.p.A.

A catalogue record for this publication is available from the British Library

ISBN 978-0521-74856-8 Student's Book
ISBN 978-0521-74857-5 Teacher's Book
ISBN 978-0521-74859-9 Audio CD Set (2)

Acknowledgements

The authors and publishers would like to thank the ELT professionals who commented on the material at different stages of its development:

ABC Pathways School, Hong Kong; Klára Banks; Paul Bress; Alexander Case; Maria Angeles Tobias Cid; Julie Dawes; Margaret Fowler; Rorror Huang; Liz Bangs-Jones; Calliope Loulaki; Justyna Martin; Rosa Llopart Queraltó; Beatriz Muñiz Rodríguez; Diane Reeves; Roger Scott

The authors of the second edition would like to thank the following reviewers who commented on the first edition to help shape the second edition and reviewers who commented on the second edition: Christine Barton, Jonathan Baum, Sevim Ciftci, Philip Cordwell, Marc Danis, Marc Dennis, Elizabeth Elston, Sean Fox, Jonathan Gibbons, Ebru Gültekin, Rosalie Kerr, Begum Kirik, Rupert Procter, Gülsah Sünter, Fiona Thompson, Reyhan Yüksel

The authors are grateful to:
Niki Donnelly, Laila Friese, Sarah Brierley, Emily Robinson and Clive Rumble of Cambridge University Press

Anne Robinson would like to give special thanks to Adam Evans and Annie Marriott for their insights and inspiration on the first edition, and to so **many** teaching professionals who have inspired and given feedback along the way. Special thanks to Christina and Victoria for their help, patience and enthusiasm!

Karen Saxby would like to give special thanks to everyone she has worked with in production of YLE material. She would also like to thank her sons, Tom and William, for bringing constant fun and creative inspiration for her life and work.

Editorial work by Christine Barton.

Cover design by David Lawton

Cover illustration by Simon Stephenson, NB Illustration

Book design and page make-up by eMC Design Ltd.

The authors and publishers are grateful to the following illustrators:

Advocate Art (Chris Embleton-Hall 20, 22, 23, 50, 54, 63, 116, 118), Beehive Illustration (Tina McNaughton 70, 71, 117, 119; Pulsar Studios 8, 52, 53, 56, 60, 70, 89, 96, 107, 120, 122; Theresa Tibbetts 6, 34, 36, 38, 39, 69, 80, 81, 84, 91, 111, 113), Graham-Cameron Illustration (Bridget Dowty 31, 37, 40, 87, 110; Brett Hudson 30, 50, 62, 66, 96, 97; Pip Sampson 9, 18, 24, 35, 41, 44, 45, 55, 56, 57, 61, 67, 68, 69, 74, 75, 76, 77, 97, 102, 103, 111, 121; Emily Skinner 21, 27, 37, 49, 65, 80, 81, 96; Sarah Wimperis 6, 73, 98; Sue Woollatt 14, 15, 58, 59, 62, 64, 67, 82, 90, 92, 93, 94, 95), Sylvie Poggio Artists Agency (Laetitia Aynié 16, 38, 79, 92, 109; Andy Elkerton 11, 12, 32, 83; Melanie Sharp 10, 17, 26, 27, 28, 29, 32, 33, 46, 47, 49, 63, 72, 78, 84, 85, 99, 100, 101, 104, 105, 114, 115; Lisa Smith 34), Nigel Kitching 13, 19, 21, 25, 26, 48, 52, 61, 72, 81, 88, 95, 105, 112.

Sound recordings by TEFL Audio, London

Contents

 **Unit 1**

 *Wearing and carrying*

 A **What am I wearing?**

 b<u>e</u>lt  c_ _t  dr__ss

gl_v_s 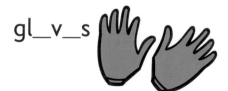 j_ck_t  t_ghts

 B **Circle the correct word.**

1 The queen is wearing a beautiful *dress* / *coat*.

2 There are *three* / *four* flags on the castle.

3 One person is carrying a big plate with *fruit* / *pasta* on it.

4 The man who's playing music is wearing funny orange *tights* / *gloves*.

5 You can see a *round* / *square* table in the castle garden.

C **CD1:02** **Who are the people at the castle? Listen and draw lines.**

Test! Listening Part 1

Mary

Peter

Robert

....

Helen

Sarah

....

Michael

Harry

 6

D **Read the sentences and write the words.**

Crossword grid:
1. b / e / l / t (vertical, "belt")

■ things we wear

□ things we carry

1 Some people wear this round the top of their trousers or skirt.

2 People put things in this and carry it on their back.

3 If it rains, you can open this so you don't get wet.

4 Some people wear this over their other clothes when they go outside.

5 We can wear these on sunny days when we don't want to wear jeans.

6 You can carry lots of clothes in this when you go on holiday.

7 Women often carry this. They put things like pens and keys in it.

8 Some girls and women wear these on their legs under their skirts.

9 We put these on our hands in cold weather.

10 Trousers often have this. You can put money in it.

11 Some children wear this at school so everyone looks the same.

 E **Write the words below the pictures. Where do we wear these on our body? Draw lines.**

1 ....a hat....

2 ....

3 ....

legs
feet
nose
head
finger
neck

4 ....

5 ....

6 ....

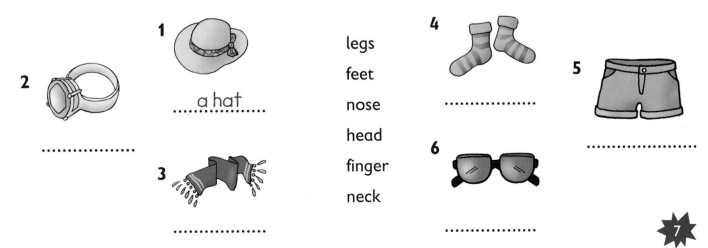

Unit 2  Spots and stripes

A Look and read. Write yes or no.  **Test!** Reading & Writing Part 2

Examples

One boy in the picture is wearing a scarf and gloves. ...yes...

A happy girl is sitting next to the person who's talking on the phone. ...no...

1 The woman who's walking with her two sons is pushing four suitcases. ....

2 The man with the beard is writing something in his newspaper. ....

3 Two of the people in the picture have got clothes with flowers on them. ....

4 One of the children who's playing on the floor has got straight hair. ....

5 The time on the clock is half past three. ....

6 The biggest plane in the picture has got its door open. ....

7 There's a boy who's listening to some music and he's taking off a striped jacket. ....

B **CD1:03** Listen and colour and draw and write.  **Test!** Listening Part 5

 8

C Talk about the flags in the first picture.

D Complete the sentences about the second picture. Use 1 or 2 words.

1 There's one boat and it's got three green flags with ....sharks............ on them.

2 The man isn't wearing .... now.

3 Two boys are walking and carrying ....

4 The girl on the boat has got .... fair hair.

5 One of the birds is carrying a green flag in its ....

6 The towel on the boy's shoulder has blue and ....

E Talk about the differences between the pictures.

F Can you find the picture I've written about?

kick	legs/feet	believe		forget	
understand		point		speak	
cry		follow		sing	
cook		watch		catch	
carry		smell		remember	
feel		shout		see	
learn		listen		whistle	
whisper		throw		hear	

B   Complete the sentences with *look*, *watch*, *listen* or *hear*.

1   Could you speak louder, please? I can't .... you.

2   .... outside! It's starting to snow!

3   Do you .... to music when you do your homework?

4   I'm going to .... the school hockey team play their game now.

C   Use a different verb from **A** to complete each question.

1   Are you noisy? Do you .....shout..... when you want to say something?

2   Are you quiet? Do you .... when you tell someone a secret?

3   Can you .... telephone numbers or must you write them down?

4   Oh dear! Do you .... people's birthdays sometimes?

5   When you don't .... in class, do you ask the teacher to explain?

D **Read the story. Choose a word from the box. Write the correct word next to numbers 1–5.**

I'm Helen. I live in the ....city...... but last August I visited my new school friend, David, who lives on a farm in the north of the country. His dad, William, is a famous (1) .... , but he's a farmer too! I saw lots of cows and other (2) .... there, but I remember Pirate, the black and white sheep dog, most.

Early one morning, David's dad came into the kitchen. 'The sheep in the west field aren't there now!' he said. 'I must find them. Come and help me!' David and I jumped up and followed him outside. We all (3) .... up into his big old green truck. Pirate jumped in too.

William drove the truck up the hill. Suddenly, Pirate got very (4) .... William stopped the truck and shouted, 'Go, Pirate! Find the sheep!' Pirate jumped out of the truck and ran behind some trees. A minute later, we saw him again. The clever dog ran round and round the sheep to make them come back down into the west field. David's dad (5) .... loudly and called, 'Well done, Pirate!'

Pirate worked very hard that day. 'He's tired,' I whispered to David after dinner. 'He ran a long way today.' But Pirate wasn't too tired to play with his ball that evening or to eat some of his favourite cookies!

Example

city	cloudy	whistled	actor	wings
climbed	animals	sausages	excited	painted

Now choose the best name for this story. Tick one box.

Pirate loses his biscuits ☐

Pirate helps on the farm ☐

Pirate drives a truck ☐

E **Play the game! Making sentences competition.**

About animals

A How do they move? Write the animals below each word.

kangaroo bat fish mouse bird crocodile goat dolphin

run	fly	jump	swim	hop
mouse	....	....	....	....
....	....	....	....	....
....	....	....	....	....
....	....	....	....	....
....	....	....	....	....

B Look and read. Choose the correct word and write it on the line.

butterflies

a camel

dinosaurs

an insect

an octopus

swans

a rabbit

1 This small animal often has brown or white fur and long ears.
   It can hop and jump very quickly.   a rabbit

2 This is usually very small and it always has six legs. Some of
   these have wings too.   ....

3 This animal carries people and heavy bags across the desert.   ....

4 These big birds are usually white. They have long necks and
   live near rivers and lakes.   ....

5 This animal lives in the sea and has eight long, curly legs.   ....

6 These have wings with lots of different colours on them.
   They fly and sit on plants and flowers.   ....

7 These animals lived a long time ago, but we only see them in
   films now because they are extinct.   ....

C Choose the right words and write them on the lines.

Dinosaurs

Example Dinosaurs ......lived...... on

our planet 150,000,000 years

ago! The first dinosaurs

1 .... like big lizards

but they had short tails, fat

2 legs .... big heads.

These dinosaurs only ate plants. Some of these

3 dinosaurs were very .... , but other

kinds of dinosaur got bigger and heavier. Some

of these started to eat meat.

4 Dinosaurs lived .... warm forests

5 where there were lots and lots ....

plants and water. But about 60,000,000 years

6 ago, ... weather on our planet

suddenly got colder and drier. Many plants

7 .... dinosaurs liked to eat disappeared,

so soon dinosaurs disappeared too.

8 People now .... dinosaur teeth in

rocks in many different parts of the world. We

9 can see .... , but only when we go to a

science museum or when we watch some films

10 .... TV. These animals are now extinct.

	living	lives	lived
1	looks	looked	looking
2	and	because	than
3	small	smaller	smallest
4	to	in	from
5	off	out	of
6	the	one	those
7	what	that	who
8	finds	found	find
9	they	their	them
10	at	by	on

D Do you know the missing word?

> lots .... dinosaurs   a story .... a dolphin

1 all kinds .... bats   **2** a book .... the jungle

3 a glass .... water   **4** this part .... the story

5 afraid .... lizards   **6** a song .... a dolphin

E Play the game! Dolphins or bats?

13

 My things

 A   **What are these? Write the words on the lines next to the pictures.**

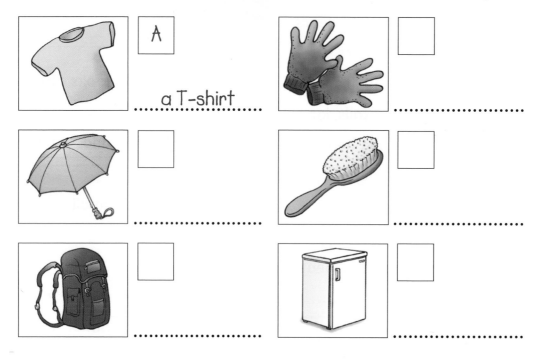

	A
	...a T-shirt...

....

....

....

....

....

 B   **Read and choose the word from A. Then complete the sentences about a brush.**

An ....

People use this in the rain. They hold it above their heads.

I carry this in my hand on wet days, then I stay dry.

If you open this when it rains, you don't get wet!

A brush

1   People use this after they ....have....... a shower. They tidy their

.... with it.

2   I brush my .... with this in .... of the mirror.

3   If you .... one of these in the morning, your .... looks

better.

C CD1:04 **Which animal picture is on each thing?**
Listen and write a letter in each box in A on page 14.

 Test! Listening Part 3

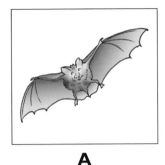

A

B

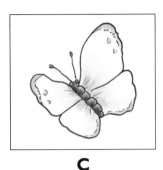

C

D

E

F

G

H

 D CD1:04 **Find and colour the two parts of the sentences.**

A Her mother bought Betty this

C Her friend Mary gave her this and

D Betty bought these when

E Her cousin Ben bought it for her because

F Betty took this with her

G Her grandma made these

she was on holiday a long time ago.

when she went camping last summer.

and she wears them when the weather is cold.

last year at the zoo.

she uses it every day.

he knows she loves these animals.

E **Find the differences.**

F **Ask and answer questions about your things.**

15

Are you called Helen?

 A **Let's talk about your friends and family.**

1 Who lives in your house?

2 Has anyone in your family got the same first name as you?

3 Who do you sit next to at school?

4 Which friends do you see at the weekend?

5 Tell me about your best friend.

 B ⊙ CD1:05 **Who came to Mary's party? Listen and write names.**

1 .... *Jane* ....   **a** has guitar lessons too.

2 ....   **b** is in the same class.

3 ....   **c** is Mary's cousin.

4 ....   **d** is Mary's best friend.

5 ....   **e** likes the same music.

6 ....   **f** is very funny.

7 ....   **g** goes sailing too.

8 ....   **h** is a loud singer.

 C **Look at the picture in D. Complete the sentences.**

1 Two people are wearing .... *glasses* ....

2 Two men have got a ....

3 Two people are .... a drink.

4 Two people are .... because they are happy.

5 Two people are reading a ....

16 6 Two people have got their eyes .... because they are sleeping.

D CD1:06 **Listen and draw lines.**

Daisy

Robert

Michael

Emma

Sarah

Peter

Fred

 E **Read the conversation and choose the best answer.**

Emma and Katy are waiting for the train. They're talking about tennis.

What does Katy say to Emma? Write a letter (A–E) for each answer.

Example

 Emma: Would you like to watch the tennis game on television this afternoon?

 Katy: ....C.........

 Emma: It begins at three o'clock.

1 **Katy:** ....

 Emma: Of course! Harry's staying with us. You can meet him too.

2 **Katy:** ....

 Emma: No. He's my favourite cousin. He plays tennis a lot too!

3 **Katy:** ....

Emma: Yes, he is!

A Who's he? Do I know him?

B Is he good at it?

C Yes, I would. What time does it start? (**Example**)

D Pardon? Can you say that again?

E Oh! But can I come before that? At half past two?

How do you spell it?

 A ee or ea?

The queen needs to see the trees this week!

Mr Feet and Miss Sleep agree to meet in Green Street!

Mr Bean's team have all got clean jeans on!

It's easy to steal each leaf!

In my dream I had a meal on the beach with a sea monster!

Tell Mrs Head that her bread is ready!

We can't carry the heavy treasure in this weather!

 B **Write the missing letters.**

br e a d   n _ _ d   cl _ _ n   qu _ _ n   t _ _ m   m _ _ l

f _ _ t   st _ _ l   tr _ _ sure   gr _ _ n   _ _ sy   m _ _ n

l _ _ f   r _ _ dy   agr _ _   tr _ _   w _ _ ther   dr _ _ m

 C 🔘 CD1:07 **Listen and circle the words you hear.**

D Read the email and write the missing words.  Write one word on each line.

Example

1

2

3

4

5

To: David

From: Sally

Hi David,

Would you ....like........ to come to my house on Monday next

week? You can come .... bus. It's easy and cheap!

The bus stop is on .... corner of my street. You can meet

my new pet. It's .... red and green parrot!

If you want you can .... a meal with us and, if the

weather's good, we can .... for a walk on the beach too!

See you soon!

Sally

E CD1:08 Listen and write the names.

Monday – *Go to Sally's house!*

1 Name: ....Sally............

2 Bus stop is in: .... Street

3 Sally's house is in: .... Road

4 Name of house: ....

5 Sally's dog's name: ....

6 Sally's new pet's name: ....

F Now do the spelling quiz!

Unit 8  School subjects

A Write *a, e, i, o* or *u*.

A̲ r t   G _ _ g r _ p h y   H _ s t _ r y   S p _ r t

L _ n g _ _ g _ s   M _ t h s   M _ s _ c   S c _ _ n c _

B **Look and read. Choose the correct words from A and write them on the lines.**

1   Your teacher helps you to understand the past in this lesson.   ....

2   If you like learning about numbers you should study this subject.   ....

3   When you study this subject you learn about rivers and mountains. ....

C **Complete these sentences for Art.**

1   Your teacher helps you to .... in this lesson.

2   If you like .... you should study this subject.

3   When you study this subject you learn ....

D **Write sentences for two other subjects.**

1   ....

2   ....

E  **Listen and write. There is one example.**

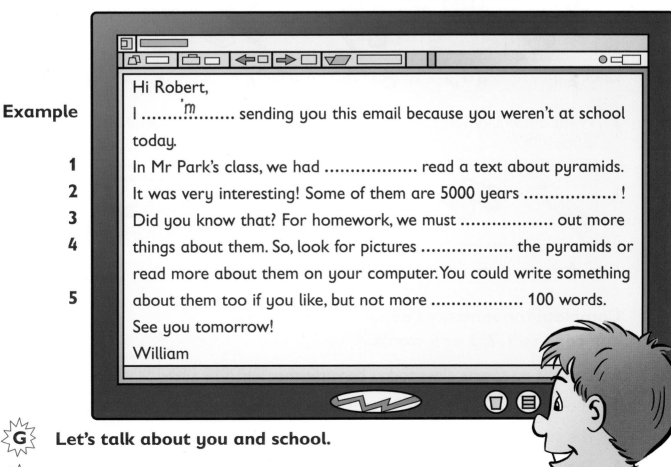

	Monday
Example	Meet in the town ....square..........
1	See art by Alex ....
2	Bus number ....
3	Look for books about ....
4	Tell Mum and Dad to come at ....
5	For lunch, take some ....

F **Read the email and write the missing words. Write one word on each line.** Test! Reading & Writing Part 7

Hi Robert,

I ....'m......... sending you this email because you weren't at school today.

1 In Mr Park's class, we had .... read a text about pyramids.

2 It was very interesting! Some of them are 5000 years .... !

3 Did you know that? For homework, we must .... out more

4 things about them. So, look for pictures .... the pyramids or read more about them on your computer. You could write something

5 about them too if you like, but not more .... 100 words.

See you tomorrow!

William

G **Let's talk about you and school.**

H **Answer the questions. Then choose the best answers for the conversation.**

 A **Find the two halves of the sentences.**

1 Glue: When you break something in two pieces,	**a** you use them to cut things like paper or thin plastic.
2 Scissors: They are usually made of metal and	**b** use this to find out what it means.
3 A dictionary: When you don't understand a word,	**c** use it to put the two halves back together again.
4 A bin: When something is old and you don't want it,	**d** use these to see how clever their students are!
5 Exams: Teachers in schools, colleges and universities	**e** use this to throw it away!

 B CD1:10 **Listen and tick (✔) the box.**

1 What will be the first lesson today?

A ☐   **B** ✔   **C** ☐

2 What should the students take to their art class?

A ☐   **B** ☐   **C** ☐

3 What did William forget to bring to school?

A ☐   **B** ☐   **C** ☐

4 Where can the students leave their dictionaries?

A ☐   **B** ☐   **C** ☐

 C **Complete the sentences about William's class.**
You can use 1, 2, 3 or 4 words.

1 There is no sports class today because the ....sports teacher.... is not well.

2 Their .... teacher is called Mr Jones.

3 The students should bring glue for tomorrow's .... class.

4 They do not need to bring pencils, erasers or .... tomorrow.

5 William remembered to bring his books and .... to school.

6 The teacher tells the class to put their dictionaries on the .... by the cupboard.

D **Listen and complete this information about your class.**

Name/teacher?	....
How many desks/class?	....
Who/sit next to?	....
What/wear?	....
Lesson easy/difficult?	....

E **Ask questions about Michael's class.**

Name/teacher?	....
How many/desks?	....
What/studying?	....
What/wear?	....
Lesson easy/difficult?	....

F **.............. 's class.**

Name/teacher?	....
How many/desks?	....
What/studying?	....
What/wear?	....
Lesson easy/difficult?	....

G **Let's do a pair dictation!**

Unit 10 Planets

A Complete the sentences about the picture.

1 An astronaut has jumped off the top of the ....stairs.......... .

2 Two of the astronauts are playing .... near the strange tree.

3 The rocket door is .... now.

4 A robot with a square .... is watching TV inside the rocket.

5 There are three more planets in the picture. One of them is .... than the other two.

6 The trees have got leaves that look like .... hands.

7 The .... on this planet looks like sand.

(stairs)	dark	open	game	bigger	head
later	golf	little	ground	air	

B Find the differences.

24

Read the text. Choose the right words and write them on the lines.

Test! Reading & Writing Part 6

Our planet

		which	where	that
Example	The planet ....where.... we live is near seven			
1	other planets. Until .... twentieth	**1** a	one	the
2	century we didn't have maps	**2** to	of	at
3	our planet. Now, we can .... pictures	**3** take	taken	took
	of it from space. These pictures are very			
4	important .... , for example, they tell	**4** because	than	or
	us what the weather is going to be like. The			
5	photos .... also very beautiful. From	**5** being	was	are
6	space, our planet .... like a blue ball	**6** look	looking	looks
7	with white clouds. .... of our planet	**7** Most	Just	Many
8	.... water on it. This water is very	**8** had	have	has
	important for all the people, animals and plants			
9	that live there, because they .... to	**9** needs	needing	need
	drink it. Our planet is important. We must learn			
10	about it and look .... it very carefully.	**10** after	for	down

 D CD1:11 **Listen and write names and colour the planets.**

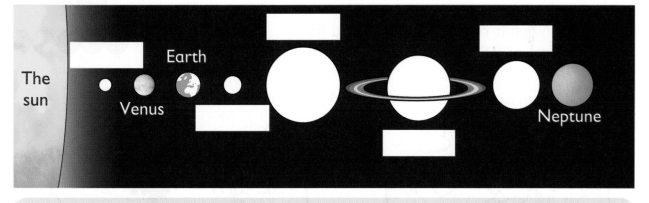

Mars   Mercury   Uranus   Saturn   Jupiter

 E **Answer questions about our planet.**

Earth			
What/colour?	blue and white	How much time/ go round the sun?	365 days, 6 hours, 16 minutes
What/temperature?	about 14 °C		
Have/rings?	no	How many/moons?	one

F **Let's find out about other planets!**

The world around us

 A **Read the sentences then complete the words in the S puzzle.**

1 This is green and you can usually find it in gardens. Cows eat it!

2 You can walk up these because they're lower than mountains.

3 You find these on farms and some farmers grow vegetables in them.

4 This is usually yellow. It's under your feet when you walk on the beach.

5 People live and work in these places. They're like towns but smaller.

6 You see these on all kinds of plants. They sometimes fall off trees.

7 You can find hundreds of tall trees in this place.

8 There is water all round this place. You need a boat to get to it.

9 These are beautiful. You can find them on the beach or at the bottom of the sea.

10 When it rains, this is grey and has lots of clouds in it.

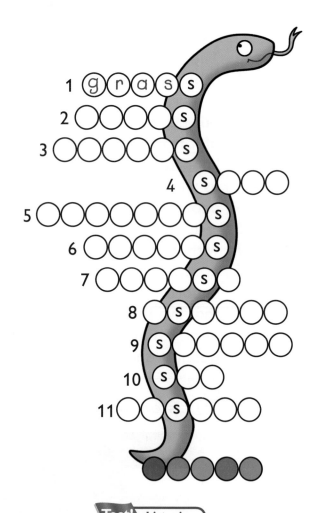

1 g r a s s
2 ○○○○ s
3 ○○○○ s
4 s ○○○
5 ○○○○○○ s
6 ○○○○○ s
7 ○○○○ s
8 ○ s ○○○○
9 ○ s ○○○
10 ○ s ○○
11 ○○ s ○○○

B **CD1:12** **Listen and colour and draw and write.** **Test!** Listening Part 5

Hill

26

C **What is the girl saying to her friend on the phone?**
Choose the best answer.

.... **calls** ....

Example Hello! How are you?
.... B ....

1 Where are you now?
....

2 Who else is there with you?
....

3 Are there any animals there?
....

4 Where do you sleep at night?
....

5 What's the weather like?
....

6 .... ?
....

A I'd like to take the dog for a walk.
B I'm fine, thanks! (**Example**)
C My parents and my uncle.
D It's hot and sunny.

E Our beds are in big tents.
F No, it was sunny in my father's field.
G We're in Yellow Hill Desert.
H Yes! I rode a camel today!

D **What's in each rucksack?**

gloves   sweater
map   hat
T–shirt   camera
shorts   dictionary
hot chocolate
torch   sunglasses
phone   umbrella
cold water

E **Play the game! Moving dictation.**

 A Find the weather words.

warmcloudswetwindydryrainhotsunnystormfoggysnowcoldicerainbowtemperature

B Choose the correct words from **A** and write them on the lines.

1 You see these in the sky and they're usually big and grey if

it's raining. ....*clouds*..............

2 You sometimes see one of these in the sky after it rains. It

has seven colours. ....

3 Stay inside when there's one of these because the rain and

wind outside are usually terrible! ....

4 If there's lots of this, it's a good day to fly a kite or go sailing. ....

5 You can see this on the top of water when it's very cold.

People like skating on it. ....

C (CD1:13) Listen. Use words from **A** to complete the sentences.

1 The friends can't play tennis if it ....*rains*........... .

2 Daisy is telling her friend about the .... last night. It was so loud

that she couldn't sleep.

3 The mother and her son think that the .... is beautiful.

4 If the .... is below zero, there might be .... on the ground.

5 It's dangerous to drive quickly in the ....

Complete this sentence:

If it snows, we can ....

D Look at the pictures. Find the differences.

 E 🔘 CD1:14 **Listen to the first half of the story.**
What did you hear about the first picture?

Now listen to the sentences about the second picture and answer these questions.

1	Which person is cold?	(Sue)	Robert	Michael	Vicky
2	Which person is wet?	Sue	Robert	Michael	Vicky
3	Who didn't bring an umbrella today?	Sue	Robert	Michael	Vicky
4	Whose house can they go to?	Sue's	Robert's	Michael's	Vicky's

 F 🔘 CD1:15 **Listen to the next part of the story. Which picture is it?**

 G Now finish the story for the other picture.

 A Look and read. Choose the correct words and write them on the lines. There is one example.

Example You eat it when you haven't got much time or when you aren't very hungry. .....a snack.....

salt

1 This is usually white and some people put it in their coffee with a spoon. ....

a picnic

2 You can skate on this or put it in a cold drink. ....

meals

3 This is usually made from fruit and you can eat it with bread and butter. ....

a plate

chocolate

4 To make this, you mix different vegetables in a big bowl. You don't have to cook them. ....

jam

5 This is white and comes from the sea. Some people put it on their food before they eat it. ....

vegetables

flour

6 Onions, potatoes and carrots are examples of this kind of food. ....

a snack

sugar

7 This is brown or white and you can make things like bread or pizzas with it. ....

a salad

8 This is very sweet and lots of people love eating it. It's usually brown. ....

pasta

ice

9 Breakfast, lunch and supper are all examples of these. ....

sandwiches

10 People enjoy having these in the countryside or at the beach. It's food that you take with you. ....

fries

 B Read the sentence. What am I making – pasta, sandwiches or fries?

1 You can make this at home with eggs and flour, but I bought this in a shop. Get some hot water ready. Put it into the water and cook it for between five and nine minutes.

....

2 To make these, you put food like salad, eggs or jam between two pieces of bread. They are usually cold, but some people like making hot ones with cheese or meat inside.

....

Now complete the sentences about the other food.

3 To make these, you need .... , which you .... into thin pieces and .... People eat them with food like ....

....

C  **Listen and tick (✔) the box.**

1 What can Betty have for dinner?

A ☐   B ☐   C ☐

2 What did David have for lunch?

A ☐   B ☐   C ☐

3 What does Katy want for breakfast?

A ☐   B ☐   C ☐

4 What did Tony eat at the party?

A ☐   B ☐   C ☐

D **Read the sentences and write the missing words.**
Write one word on each line.

How often do you ...	never	sometimes	every day	points
1 ......do...... sport?	a	b	c	....
2 eat different .... of fruit and vegetables?	a	b	c	....
3 go .... bed very late?	a	b	c	....
4 have drinks with sugar .... them?	a	b	c	....
5 eat chocolate and sweets?	a	b	c	....
6 eat foods .... burgers, chips or sausages?	a	b	c	....
7 walk .... the stairs when you could use a lift?	a	b	c	....
8 drink four glasses or more .... water a day?	a	b	c	....
9 .... breakfast?	a	b	c	....
10 watch TV for more .... two hours a day?	a	b	c	....

Now read the sentences again. Choose a, b or c.

E **Let's do a food project!**

A 🔘 CD1:17 **Listen and draw lines. There is one example.**

Paul   Anna   William   Richard

Jill   Harry   Vicky   May

B **Read the text. Choose the right words and write them on the lines.**

Swans

Test! Reading & Writing Part 6

	Swans are the biggest water birds			
Example	........in........ the world. You often see	in	of	on
1	.... on lakes in zoos or parks. Most	1 it	us	them
2	swans are white but you can	2 too	also	yet
	find black swans. They look beautiful but			
3	you should be careful .... you go	3 and	because	if
	near swans. They are very strong and can			
4	.... a man's arm! Their necks are	4 break	breaks	breaking
5	.... than any other bird's. They use	5 longest	longer	long
6	their necks to look .... food under	6 after	to	for
7	the water. They eat grass and	7 other	others	another
	plants from the bottom of the lake. Swans live			
	together in families. Young swans begin to fly			
	when they are about two months old. They			
8	usually .... with their parents until	8 staying	stays	stay
	their parents have more baby swans. Swans			
	don't like very hot or cold environments so in			
9	winter .... usually fly to warmer	9 it	they	we
	places. Swans can live for twenty years.			
10	.... they live in places like zoos,	10 There	When	Then
	they might live for fifty years!			

C **Ask and answer questions.**

32

D **Let's do the animal quiz!**

ANIMAL QUIZ

Read the questions and circle or write the correct answers.

1 Why do African elephants have big ears?
   a   To hear better
   b   To help them live in hot countries
   c   To fly

2 What is the biggest animal in the world?
   a   the African elephant
   b   the blue whale
   c   the giraffe

3 How long has there been life on our planet?
   a   for four million years
   b   for four thousand years
   c   for four billion years

4 Whales and dolphins are big fish.   Yes ☐   No ☐

5 Can you spell  ?

....

6 And ?

....

7 Can animals live at the bottom of the ocean?   Yes ☐   No ☐

8 Can horses stand up and sleep at the same time?   Yes ☐   No ☐

9 How many legs does an insect have?
   a   6
   b   8
   c   4

10 When did dinosaurs become extinct?
   a   10 million years ago
   b   20 thousand years ago
   c   65 million years ago

Cooking, eating and picnics!

 A **Write what you can see.**

Example: This is often made of metal. You use it to cut meat. ......*a knife*......

1 Before a meal, your food is on this. It's flat and usually round. ....

2 People like drinking cold drinks from this, but be careful! It can break! ....

3 If you want to have some soup, put it in this before you eat it. ....

4 This is black. Add only a little of this to your food because it tastes hot! ....

5 You might buy milk, water or fruit juice in this. ....

6 I hold this in my hand to mix different kinds of food together. ....

7 This is white. Some people put it in the water when they cook pasta. ....

8 Some people prefer to eat food like rice or vegetables with these. ....

 B **Ask your partner the questions.**

1 Where do you usually have your meals?
2 What is on your favourite pizza?
3 Who makes the dinner in your family?
4 Who washes all the plates? Do you?
5 Which food is good to take on a picnic?

C **Look at the picture and read the story.**
Write words to complete the sentences. Use 1, 2, 3 or 4 words.

A funny, short holiday

Betty West likes being a secretary, but when it's hot and sunny she looks out of the window and dreams of holidays in the countryside. Betty loves being outside! Last Thursday, the weather was beautiful. But Betty had lots of work to do that morning. She turned on her computer and started writing all the important letters on her desk.

At twelve o'clock she said to Helen, the other secretary in the room, 'We need a holiday! But we can't leave the office. What shall we do?' Helen stood up and opened the big office window. 'Let's have a holiday here!' she said. 'Turn off the computers!'

The warm light from the sun came through the open window. The two women moved their desks and put a blanket from the office cupboard on the floor. Helen fetched two glasses and a cold bottle of lemonade from the office kitchen and put a box of cookies from her bag on a big white plate. Then Helen played a CD that had birdsong music on it.

The two women sat on the blanket, had their picnic, closed their eyes and dreamed of their holidays. It was difficult to start work again that afternoon! When Betty got home her husband asked, 'Did you have a good day?' 'Yes! I wrote 48 letters,' she laughed. 'But I went on holiday too!'

Examples

Betty likes her job. She's a ....secretary........ .

Betty looks out of the window when it's ....hot and sunny..... outside.

Questions

1 Last week, the .... was very good on Thursday.

2 Betty had to write lots of .... that morning.

3 Another secretary called .... worked in the office too.

4 At twelve o'clock, Helen and Betty .... their computers.

5 Helen went to the office kitchen to get a .... and some glasses.

6 The women listened to music that sounded like ....

7 When Helen arrived home she said, 'I .... today, but I wrote lots of letters too!'

D **Let's play a guessing game!**

What do they do?

A Look at the pictures. Write the jobs.

(1) (2) (3) (4)

(5) (6) (7)

Crossword grid:
- 6 across/down: d
- 1: m
- 3: p
- 5: s
- 4: j
- 2: c
- 7: c

B Read the sentences. Write the jobs from the crossword.

1 I take pictures of places and people for magazines. ...... a photographer ......

2 I find out about things that happen and write about them for newspapers. ....

3 This person works in an office, answers the phone and uses a computer to write emails and letters. ....

4 I work in a restaurant. I make meals for the people who come here to eat. ....

5 You go to see these people if you are ill. They look at you and give you medicine. ....

6 You take your car to this person when you have a problem with it. ....

7 We work in a theatre. People come and see us and they can also watch us on TV. ....

C **CD1:18** Listen and write the numbers of the pictures in A.

A .... B .... C .... D ....

D Which of the jobs in A do you like best? Which would you NOT like to do? Write the jobs next to the numbers.

7 = the best **1** = the worst

7 .... 6 .... 5 .... 4 ....

3 .... 2 .... 1 ....

E CD1:19 **What did Sarah take to each place?**

Listen and write a letter in each box. There is one example.

letters B

a map ☐

a scarf ☐

an umbrella ☐

a jacket ☐

a camera ☐

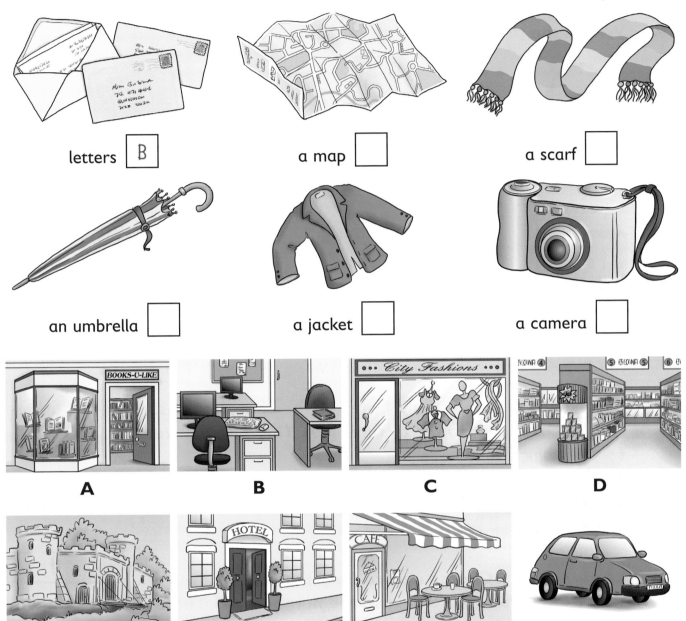

A BOOKS-U-LIKE

B

C City Fashions

D

E

F HOTEL

G CAFE

H

F **Sarah talks to a famous TV star.**

Our journalist Sarah talks to John Clock!

My sister's an engineer

 A What's the time?

a  `1`

.......3 o'clock.......

....

b ☐

....

....

c 16:00 ☐

....

....

d 19:15 ☐

....

....

e 09:45 ☐

....

....

f ☐

....

....

 B  CD1:20 **Read the questions. Listen to the conversations. Write 2–4 in the boxes next to the pictures in A. There is one example.**

1 What time is lunch today?
2 What time does the television programme begin?
3 What time does Ann have to get up for school?
4 What time is it now?

 C **Read the story. Choose a word from the box.** **Write the correct word next to the numbers 1–5. There is one example.**

Test! Reading & Writing Part 4

Michael is in London. He flew there last week with some school friends. They're having English lessons at a college. He's talking to the other people in his ......*family*...... on one of the college computers. His father, Jim, teaches (1) .... and he's at home now. His mother, Mary, is a businesswoman. She's visiting a (2) .... in China where they make mobile phones and watches. His sister, Emma, is in another country too. She's (3) .... with her class in the mountains!

Michael's family had to think carefully about a good time to talk to each other because the time is different in each of the four countries. Michael can ⁽⁴⁾ .... the computer room in London at 4 pm. His dad doesn't turn on their computer at home until 7 pm. Emma can use the computer in the hotel at 5 pm after skiing. But it's ⁽⁵⁾ .... for Michael's mother. For her, their computer conversation is at 1 am!

Example

family   spending   difficult   art   hour   factory   fast   skiing   fetch   use

Now choose the best name for this story. Tick one box.

Emma's funny day at the airport ☐

Michael's family conversation ☐

A lesson for Michael's dad ☐

D 🔘 CD1:21 **Listen and tick (✔) the box. There is one example.**

Example   What's Kim's job?

A ✔   B ☐   C ☐

1   How does Kim go to work?

A ☐   B ☐   C ☐

2   What time does Kim start work?

A ☐   B ☐   C ☐

3   Where does Kim have lunch?

A ☐   B ☐   C ☐

4   What was Kim's first job?

A ☐   B ☐   C ☐

5   What does Kim like most about her job?

A ☐   B ☐   C ☐

E **Play the game! Which job have I drawn?**

39

My day at work

A Read the text and write the missing words. Write one word on each line.

Example	David is 44. He's ....*a*.......... policeman. He works
1	at the police .... , which is in the city. Every
2	day he gets up at six o'clock and .... on his
	uniform. He wears a blue hat, a blue jacket and trousers.
3	When he arrives .... work, he talks to the other
	policemen who have worked during the night. Then he
	leaves the police station and goes out into the city. He tries
4	.... stop traffic problems. Sometimes David helps
	people when they have lost things. Sometimes he catches
5	people .... have stolen things.

B Choose a job and complete the boxes.

Name: ....

What/job?	....
When/get up?	....
Uniform?	....
Where/work?	....
Age?	....

Name: ....

What/job?	....
When/get up?	....
Uniform?	....
Where/work?	....
Age?	....

C   Put together the text about Emma the firewoman.

D   An afternoon at the fire station. Listen to Jim.
        Write numbers 1–4 in the boxes next to the pictures.

This is me coming down from the
fire station to the ....
on a big piece of ....
I had a lot of fun!

This is us .... the fire station.
We're wearing fireman hats – my
teacher has got a hat on too! And I'm
putting a fireman's .... on, but
it's too big!

Now we're very ....
because we're playing with the
water from the ....
....

This is Miss Night and our ......_class_......... .
We're outside the ....
.... but the ....
is very hot.

E   Complete the sentences under the pictures with words from the box.

> **Example**
>   class   wet   walk   jacket   ground   fire station   weather
>   fire engine   inside   fire   plastic   work   traffic   police car

 A **Read the story. Choose a word from the box.**
Write the correct word next to numbers 1–5. There is one example.

Daisy Brown had a little brother called David who made her angry! David was only five but he never, never stopped asking questions! 'How does a .....light..... turn on and off, Daisy? When did the first planes fly, Aunt Sally? Why can dogs (1) .... some sounds better than I can, Grandpa?' He sometimes asked very difficult questions. 'How old is our planet, Mum? Why have tigers got (2) .... bodies, Daisy?' People usually said, 'I don't know, David!'

One day, Dad, Daisy and David were (3) .... in the town when David pointed to the new science museum and asked, 'What's that (4) .... , Daisy?' Daisy didn't know, but their father did. He smiled. 'It's a museum. We might find lots of answers to your questions there.' Daisy (5) .... going to museums. She turned to David and said, 'Let's go there now! What shall we find out about first?' That was a difficult question for David. 'I don't know!' he said!

Example

light   hear   candy   deciding   end   place   loved   striped   half   shopping

(6) **Now choose the best name for the story. Tick one box.**

Daisy's favourite animals ☐

David's difficult questions ☐

Dad's visit to town ☐

B **Listen and colour the museum picture in A.**

C Write the question words on the lines.

D Choose questions for different people.

How many   How much   How often   How old   What   What time
When   ~~Where~~   Which   Who   Whose   Why   How

Name	Your name ....
	Example ....Where........ do you live?
....	**1** .... is your surname?
....	**2** .... is the cleverest student in this class?
....	**3** .... did you come to school today? By bus?
....	**4** .... birthday is in April?
....	**5** .... are you? 10? 11?
....	**6** .... did you get up this morning? Seven o'clock?
....	**7** .... homework do you have every day? Too much?
....	**8** .... people live in your house? Four? Five?
....	**9** .... sport do you like best?
....	**10** .... do you listen to music? Every day?
....	**11** .... will you go home? Soon?
....	**12** .... are you learning English?

E Write questions! Answer questions!

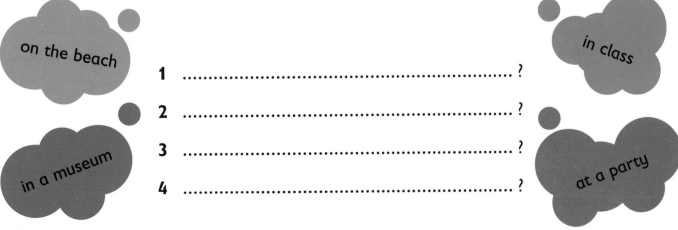

on the beach

in class

1 .... ?

2 .... ?

3 .... ?

4 .... ?

in a museum

at a party

F Play the game! Questions mingle.

43

Picture differences

A **Look at these pictures. Answer questions.**

1  2 3 4  5

B **Find these people in C. Answer the questions.**

1  2 3 4  5

1 Where is this person?	**3** What is she/he doing?
2 What kind of hair has she/he got?	**4** What is she/he wearing?

C **Look at picture a and read. Write yes or no.**

Test! Reading & Writing Part 2

a

Examples	All the people are sitting down.	.......yes......
	One of the children is playing with a robot.	.......no......
1	Most of the people who are outside the café are young children.	....
2	There are enough green chairs for everyone to sit on.	....
3	The tables are all round and are all the same colour.	....
4	The blue bicycle that's next to the café has fallen over.	....
5	More than one person is wearing trousers with white stripes on them.	....
6	One of the grown ups is using a pen to write a letter to a friend.	....
7	The sky is a funny colour and is full of clouds.	....

D **How is picture b different?**

b

Example

> A woman is wearing a green jacket. A woman *isn't* wearing a green jacket.
> She's wearing a *yellow* jacket.

 E **Read the conversation and choose the best answer.**
Write a letter (A–H) for each answer. You do not need
to use all the letters. There is one example.

Katy is talking to her dad, Harry, about the letter she's writing.

Example 🧑 **Harry:** Who are you writing to, Katy?

👧 **Katy:** .... *E* ....

Questions

1 🧑 **Harry:** I remember him! Is he on holiday?

👧 **Katy:** ....

2 🧑 **Harry:** Wow! When did he leave?

👧 **Katy:** ....

3 🧑 **Harry:** What does he do each day?

👧 **Katy:** ....

4 🧑 **Harry:** That sounds interesting. Where's he staying?

👧 **Katy:** ....

5 🧑 **Harry:** Great! Would you like to do that next year?

👧 **Katy:** ....

A About two weeks ago, I think.

B They didn't make any friends there.

C With an English family who've got a big flat.

D Perhaps! I don't know yet.

E My friend Richard, the boy who I play tennis with.

F No, because I only need a stamp.

G They have lessons in the morning, then visit museums.

H Yes! He's studying English in London.

 At the hospital

 A   **Look and read. Find the words in the box.**

Example   When you have this, your nose goes red and you might have a cough.

1   An ambulance takes you to this place if you are very ill.

2   You go to see this person if you've got toothache.

3   If you feel ill, the doctor gives you this to make you better.

4   You go there to buy medicine and you can sometimes buy other things like soap and combs there, too.

5   These people look after people who are ill in hospital.

6   This often has a light on top and can take you to hospital.

a	h	o	s	p	i	t	a	l	t	a
t	e	m	p	e	r	a	t	u	r	e
p	a	c	h	e	m	i	s	t	s	m
a	n	a	m	b	u	l	a	n	c	e
n	r	f	e	r	c	l	c	h	r	d
u	u	g	a	o	k	m	o	u	y	i
r	q	v	w	k	y	o	l	r	b	c
s	i	j	x	e	b	z	d	t	d	i
e	a	d	e	n	t	i	s	t	i	n
s	t	o	m	a	c	h	a	c	h	e

B    **Listen and draw lines. There is one example.**   Test! Listening Part 1

Michael

John

Katy

William

Betty

Sarah

Mary

C   **Complete the sentences with other words from the box in A.**

1   .... , the boy in the white shorts, has .... his arm.

2   .... , the girl in the striped T–shirt, has got a .... leg.

3   .... , the boy in the red jacket, has got a ....

4   .... , the girl in the purple trousers, might have a ....

5   .... , the little girl with the white T–shirt, has started to ....

D **Read the conversation and choose the best answer.**

Example

Doctor Wall: Good morning, William. I'm Doctor Wall. What's the matter?

William: ....H..................

1 Doctor Wall: When did you start to feel like this?

William: ....

2 Doctor Wall: What did you eat yesterday evening?

William: ....

3 Doctor Wall: I see. Was it a chocolate cake?

William: ....

4 Doctor Wall: Happy birthday for yesterday!

William: ....

5 Doctor Wall: No, you don't. Why don't you go home and lie down?
And don't eat any more chocolate cake!

William: ....

A Four pieces of pizza and a lot of birthday cake.

B It hurt when I woke up this morning.

C I won't. I'm not hungry today!

D Lots of my school friends came to my house.

E Yes. Mum always makes that cake for me on my birthday.

F I started school when I was five years old.

G Thank you. Do I need to take any medicine?

H I've got a stomach-ache. (**Example**)

 E **Ask and answer questions about Doctor Wall and Mrs Ring's jobs.**

Job?	Doctor
When/work?	every night
Name/hospital?	Sky hospital
Where/hospital?	Station Road
New/old?	new

Job?	Ambulance driver
When/work?	every weekend
Name/hospital?	Swan hospital
Where/hospital?	Park Square
New/old?	old

 A How many words can you find on the calendar page?

SEPTEMBER

1	2	3 a week	4 hours	5	6	7 midnight	8	9 summer	10
11 a weekend	12	13	14 a year	15	16 midday	17 days	18	19	20 a century
21	22 months	23	24	25 minutes	26	27 a diary	28 winter	29	30

Write the blue words on the line:

shortest time > minutes,

.... > longest time

 B Choose the correct words from **A** and write them on the lines.

Example There are usually 365 days in one of these but
sometimes it has 366 days! ....a year............

1 People write about what happened during the day in this. ....

2 Lots of people like this part of the year because the
weather is usually hot and sunny. ....

3 You can say twelve o'clock like this if it's the end of the
morning. ....

4 There are sixty of these in each hour. ....

5 Twenty–four of these make one day. ....

6 This is another way to say Saturday and Sunday. ....

7 There are twelve of these in a year. ....

8 A new one of these begins every hundred years. ....

9 This is usually the coldest part of the year and
sometimes it snows. ....

10 This is the end of the day and another way to say
twelve o'clock. ....

C Put the words in the correct box. There is one example.

baby animals   making a snowman   making a sandcastle on the beach   leaves falling
camping   starting school   cold   wet   finishing school   flies   flowers   hot   skiing
warm   picnics   soup   bears sleeping   January   April   December   July
August   February   March   June   September   May   November   October

spring	summer	autumn (fall)	winter
			cold
....	....	....	....
....	....	....	....
....	....	....	....
....	....	....	....
....	....	....	....
....	....	....	....
....	....	....	....
....	....	....	....
....	....	....	....

 D   **Talk about how the pictures are different.**   Test! Speaking Part 1

A

B

 E   **Read the diary and write the missing words.**   Test! Reading & Writing Part 7
Write one word on each line.

Sunday, 28 April

Example   I rode ....to........ Appletree Forest today with Dad and two friends

1   who are .... Harry and Sarah. We made boats from an

2   old newspaper and sailed .... best one down the river

3   first. The paper soon got wet but the boat moved fast ....

  it was windy today. Later, I caught four fish. Dad made a fire with

4   some wood .... Harry fetched from under the trees and we

5   .... some onions on the fire for our lunch! They tasted great!

  I had lots of fun today.

 F   **Play time games!**

Important numbers

How old are you today?

Today, I am [ ] years [ ] months [ ] days old!

A How long / tall / high / far away?

  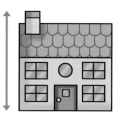 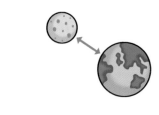 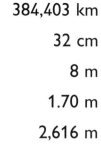

384,403 km

32 cm

8 m

1.70 m

2,616 m

B Who is the youngest and oldest?

Example
1
Did you ....know....... that the youngest driver in the world passed his test .... 27 March 1974 when he was 14 years 235 days old! The youngest golfer to
2
hit a golf ball all the way to the flag .... called Matthew Draper. Matthew hit the ball 112 metres,
3
.... he was only 5 years 212 days old when he
4
.... that! Sydney Ling was only 13 when he
5
wrote, ... also filmed, the famous movie, Lex the Wonderdog, in 1973. The film was 92 minutes
6
.... !
7
.... oldest person to fly in a plane was Charlotte Hughes. Her 110th birthday present was a ticket to fly .... London to New York but she
8
9
.... again when she was 115! Harry Stevens was the oldest person in the world to get married.
10
Harry, the new husband, was 103 and .... new wife was already 84!

C Choose the right words and write them on the lines in B.

Example   know   knew   knowing

1   in   on   at
2   be   were   was
3   but   or   if
4   doing   does   did
5   when   and   after

6   long   longer   longest
7   An   The   Any
8   from   off   for
9   flies   flew   fly
10   her   your   his

D Write sentences. Use one number and two words.

```
365        12
    60
100        24
```

months   hours
days   minutes
century   years
hour   year   day

1   There are 365 days in a year. ....
2   ....
3   ....
4   ....
5   ....

E Complete the shortest to the longest sentences with your numbers.

I'm .... metres tall.
My favourite number is ....
My telephone number is ....
My birthday is on ....
I often take the number .... bus.
It takes .... minutes to come to school.
My school is .... kilometres from my house.
About .... people live in my village/town/city.

F Do the birthday puzzle!

Unit 24

A **Choose the correct words and complete the sentences.**

buy   ride   at   astronauts   by   phone   space
plane   get   flies   legs   city   driver   problems

1 **a helicopter** A pilot sometimes ....flies........ this to get quickly to people who are having ...problems... .

2 **a train** You wait .... stations for this and when it arrives, you .... on it.

3 **rockets** .... go into .... in these but sometimes these go to other planets without any people inside them.

4 **a taxi** You can .... someone and ask them to send a .... to take you to different places in one of these.

5 **a bicycle** You use your .... to make this move then you can go for a .... on it!

6 **a ticket** You need to .... one of these when you go .... bus or plane.

7 **an airport** People go to this place when they want to go to another .... by ....

B CD1:24 **Listen to the sentences about picture 1. Write how picture 2 is different.**

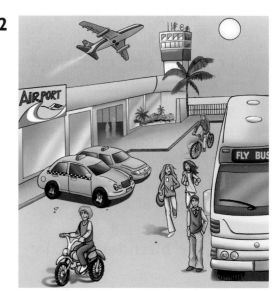

52

Example In my picture, the man on the motorbike has got curly hair.

C **Which words mean the same as the underlined words? Draw lines.**

1 We <u>arrived at</u> the restaurant at six.

2 Mum <u>drove me</u> to the party.

3 You can <u>take</u> the number 7 bus.

4 My uncle's a <u>truck</u> driver.

5 I <u>walk</u> to school.

6 We <u>flew</u> to the island.

A go on foot

B catch

C took me in the car

D lorry

E went by plane

F got to

 D 🔘 **CD1:25** **How did Richard get to each place?**

Test! Listening Part 3

Listen and write a letter in each box. There is one example.

 G

A

B

C

D

E

F

 E **Answer Sally's questions about Richard's week. Write 1, 2, 3 or 4 words.**

G   **H**

1 Sally: Why did Richard go to the airport?

John: He went there to meet <u>an important person</u> .

2 Sally: What's the quickest way to get to the museum?

John: Going to the museum .... is the quickest.

3 Sally: Where did Richard lose his money?

John: He dropped it .... when he was riding there on his bike.

4 Sally: Did Richard enjoy his ride in the helicopter?

John: Of course he did! He was .... in the air and the lorries below him looked very little!

5 Sally: Did Richard go to any places which weren't for work?

John: Yes. On Tuesday, he tried a new restaurant which is .... in town. The food and the ride there were great!

What are they going to do?

A Listen and write **yes** or **no**.

1 .....yes.....

2 ....

3 ....

4 ....

5 ....

6 ....

7 ....

8 ....

B You have eight questions.

C CD1:26 Listen and write ten things to take on holiday.

Example .....pens.....

1	6 ....
2	7 ....
3	8 ....
4	9 ....
5	10 ....

D Look at the picture and read the story.

Mary's naughty friend

Mary was too excited to eat her dinner. She suddenly jumped up from the table and said, 'I'm going to phone Grandma before I go on holiday with the school!'

Mary's grandmother was a little surprised to hear her granddaughter on the phone. 'It's very late, Mary. Why aren't you in bed?' 'Because I'm excited,' Mary answered. 'I'm going to have lots of fun with my friend from school. We're going on holiday tomorrow!' 'What are you going to do?' her grandmother asked.

'Well, we have to take pens and write about the birds we see there, but my friend and I are going to look for a big, dark cave with bats and a furry mountain monster inside!' Mary said.

'That's very brave of you,' Grandma laughed. 'What else?' 'Well, we have to take things for washing,' Mary answered. 'But my friend and I are going to wash outside. We can clean our dirty faces in the rain! And we have to take things for eating, like forks and spoons, but my friend and I are going to put sweets and chocolate biscuits in our rucksacks and have snacks in the night. And we're going to put an ugly plastic spider in Richard White's bed!'

'Who is this naughty friend of yours, Mary?' Grandma asked. 'I'm not going to tell you that, Grandma,' Mary answered. 'It's a secret!'

E Write some words to complete the sentences. You can use 1, 2, 3 or 4 words.

Examples Mary couldn't ....._eat her dinner_.... because she was too excited.
She left the table and went to phone her ...._grandma_....

Questions

1 Mary's grandma was .... when Mary phoned her.

2 Mary and her friend are going to look for .... that's big and dark.

3 Mary and her friend want to find bats and .... in the cave.

4 Grandma thinks Mary and her friend are ....

5 Mary says, 'We're going to wash .... in the rain!'

6 Mary and her friend are going to eat .... in the night.

7 Mary can't tell her grandmother her friend's name because it's a
.... !

F Play the game! Categories.

A Write the words under the correct verb.

a suitcase	hotels	cities	motorbike	car
a rucksack ...1...	a torch	shops	bus	a camera
an apartment	money	plane	a park	taxi
a tent	train	bicycle	a map	museums

carry / go by / stay in / take / visit

B Listen and write numbers after the green words in A.

C Helen and her new friend Ben are talking about Helen's holidays.
Read the conversation and choose the best answer.
Write a letter (A–H) for each answer.
There is one example.

Test! Reading & Writing Part 3

Example

Ben: This is our last week at school.

Helen: ....C..........

Questions

1 Ben: Where do you usually go on holiday?

Helen: ....

2 Ben: Me too. Do you stay in a hotel?

Helen: ....

3 Ben: So, you have to take lots of things with you, then!

Helen: ....

4 Ben: What do you do during the day?

Helen: ....

5 Ben: This year, I'm going to London for my holidays.

Helen: ....

A My best holiday was two years ago.

B No, only to the beach for two weeks.

C Yes, I know. Our holidays start on Monday! (**example**)

D We climb, have picnics and swim in the river too.

E The tent, some maps and food, of course!

F No, we sleep in a tent in a farmer's field.

G To the mountains with my family.

H Wow! Can I come with you?

 The day we forgot our tent.

  Listen and colour and write.

Robert's holiday last summer

A Make a story with the seven pictures.

B Read the story. Choose a word from the box. Write the correct word next to the numbers 1–5. There is one example.

Test! Reading & Writing Part 4

Every summer, Robert goes to the ......beach...... with his parents, aunt, uncle and

two cousins, Katy and Sarah for a week. One afternoon last year, the children

sailed to a small island that was about a kilometre away. They took a

(1) .... with them and ate it on the rocks there.

Katy jumped up and said, 'Let's walk round the island. We might find something

exciting here!' They did! They found a big dark (2) .... where the sea

went in and out. 'Perhaps a sea monster lives here!' Robert whispered and

laughed. 'Or pirates (3) .... treasure here!' Katy said.

They spent a long time looking for shells. Then Sarah said, 'It's half past six!

Come on! We must go back!' They (4) .... round and saw a man. It was

too dark to see his face.

'It's a pirate!' said Sarah. 'No, it isn't! It's me!' Robert's dad called. 'Wow! What a

(5) .... place! But you're late! It's time to go back to the hotel.'

> **Example**
> beach   map   turned   lost   great   ready   hide   picnic   follow   cave

Now choose the best name for the story. Tick one box.

A picnic on the beach ☐

A dangerous visit to a cave ☐

What we do in the summer ☐

 C 🔘 CD1:28 **Look and draw lines.**

Robert   Michael   Betty   Katy   Sarah   Emma   Richard   Harry

 D **Complete the sentences.**

1 Two of the people in the picture have got their eyes ....*closed*........ and are sleeping.

2 There is a man sleeping inside a .... that's got stripes on it.

3 The man with the .... hit the ball and then fell on the sand.

4 The boy who wants to stop the ball has got two hands in the ....

5 The green and pink butterfly is smaller than the white butterfly with black ....

6 Four of the people in the picture are enjoying a game of ....

E **Play the game! The verb–noun chain.**

 59

An interesting job

 A **Read the story. Look at the example. Find five more words in the text which are wrong.**

1 Bill <u>tomato</u> writing stories and wants to be

2 a famous journalist like his mother one day.

3 Last Tuesday, Bill was playing in the street with his friends. Suddenly, a black

4 understood with dark windows stopped and a woman got out.

5 Bill classroom at the woman and said to his friends, 'Look. That's the queen!'

6 His friends didn't believe him. Then the woman came up to Bill and asked him,

7 'Is there a good mechanic near here?' 'Yes, there's one just round the yellow,'

8 answered Bill. 'Can you take us there?' asked the woman.

9 Bill got into the car and took them to the mechanic. 'Excuse me', he said, 'but

10 aren't you the queen?' The woman trousers, 'Yes, I am. Thank you very much

11 for helping us.' The mechanic took a photo of Bill and the queen and a week

12 later, a downstairs from the queen arrived. Bill used it with the photo to write a story for the town newspaper.

B **Where do these words go in the story?**

> likes   letter   smiled   corner   car   looked

C **Now choose the best name for this story. Tick one box.**

An important person visits our town ☐   Our car has problems ☐

A big car ☐

D **Write 1, 2, 3 or 4 words to complete each sentence.**

Example   Bill's mum is .....*a famous journalist*..... .

1 The windows of the car that stopped near Bill were ....

2 When Bill said, 'It's the queen!', his friends .... him.

3 The queen wanted to know where she could find ....

4 The queen thanked .... for helping them.

5 Someone took a picture of .... that day.

6 A week later, the postman brought Bill .... from the queen.

7 Bill wrote a story for .... about the day the queen visited the town.

E **Read the queen's diary. Write one word on each line.**

Example Earlier today I went to ....<u>visit</u>........ a new museum that was
1 about 100 kilometres away. My driver .... me there in
the car. On the way home, the car sounded strange, so we had
2 .... find a mechanic.
3 We saw a .... in the street with some friends and he
4 knew a mechanic .... worked just round the corner.
He showed us the way.
Tomorrow morning, I'll send him a letter to thank
5 him .... helping us!

F CD1:29 **Tell the story.** Test! Speaking Part 3

G **Write your answers to these questions**

1 Are you good at making things? ....

2 Do you study hard at school for all the subjects you have? ....

3 What job would you like to do in the future? ....

4 What subjects do you need to be good at? ....

5 Which jobs would you NOT like to do? ....

H **Play the game! What's my job?**

What's it made of?

A **What's this? Write the words on the lines.**

Example

We use this to make small things like keys and big things like
bridges because it's very strong.   ......metal......

1 This comes from trees. It's hard but you can cut it and make
   things like shelves or bookcases with it.   ....

2 This comes from animals like sheep. Warm clothes like
   scarves and sweaters are made with it.   ....

3 You can write or read words on this. It's usually made from
   trees and is flat and often white.   ....

4 People sometimes find this in rocks or in rivers. Expensive
   rings are often made of it.   ....

5 You can see through this so we use it to make things like
   windows, but did you know it's made from sand?   ....

B **What can you see?**

C **Put them in the boxes!**

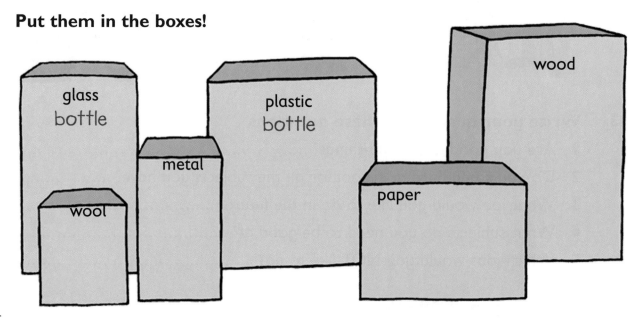

D CD1:30 **Listen and colour and draw and write.**

E **Read about glass. Choose the right words and write them on the lines.**

Glass isn't new. People made glass bowls and bottles more ......*than*...... 5,000 years

1 .... ! But no one knows who first found the secret of making glass and no

2 one knows when that ....

3 or where.

4 In one story, some men from a ship stopped on a beach .... cook some

5 food. They made a fire on the sand, but they couldn't find .... small

6 rocks to put their pot on. Someone went back to the ship .... brought

7 some small rocks from the ship to use. When .... rocks and the sand

8 got hot .... the cook's fire, they mixed together and made glass!

So the next time you look through a window .... have a glass of water, think, 'Wow, this glass is made from very, very, very hot sand!'

Example then *than* when

1 ago after already

2 happen happens happened

3 to for with

4 no any all

5 if and because

6 these this that

7 in at down

8 or but so

F **Play the game! Find things in this room.**

What's in your pockets?

A **Look at the pictures. Read the sentences. Write one word on each line.**

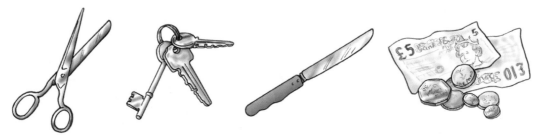

1 You find these in pockets and bags and they are usually silver and made of metal. You use them to open and close doors. ....keys...........

2 You find this in pockets and bags and it's usually made of metal or paper. You use it to buy things. ....

3 You use these to cut paper. They are usually silver and made of metal and you find them in classrooms and kitchens. ....

4 You use this to cut bread and meat. All or part of it is usually silver and made of metal. You find it in kitchens and restaurants. ....

B **Find the words in the box. You can see them all in the picture in C.**

b	i	s	c	u	t	i	z
s	u	g	a	r	m	v	c	f
n	e	w	s	p	a	p	e	r
t	j	p	a	l	g	e	l	i
i	e	m	l	a	a	p	w	d
g	a	c	t	t	z	p	m	g
h	n	u	j	e	i	e	i	e
t	s	p	o	o	n	r	l	t
s	c	o	o	k	e	r	k	k

Make sentences!
Use three words from the box.
Sentences in A will help you.

C **Look and read. Who is saying these things?**

1 How ......much...... milk would you like in your tea? | much many more

2 I don't take milk, thanks. But I'd like .... sugar! | these some any

3 Shall I put .... ice in that for her? | an some these

4 No, thanks. She never has .... ice in her drinks. | any each another

5 Would you like .... ice cream? | an those all

6 No, thank you. I don't like .... of those ice creams. | other any every

Test! Speaking Part 1

 D **Say how the pictures are different.**

 E **Read the teacher's note and colour the picture in C.**

CLASS 6

I will be 5 minutes late for the lesson today.

Look at the picture of the kitchen at the top of page 65.

Work in pairs.

1 One of you must colour four things on the left of the picture.

   One of you must colour four things on the right of the picture.

   You can choose all the colours that you use.

2 Tell each other to colour four other things in the picture. You can choose all the colours again.

Mr Wing

 F **Play the game! I know what you ate yesterday.**

 A **What's the question?**

1 <u>What do you like doing?</u>...

Playing exciting computer games, of course!

2 ....

Let me think! A big piece of that lovely banana cake, please!

3 ....

Can I have some apple juice?

4 ....

I think it's a boring film. It's very long too.

5 ....

That's easy! I love listening to my favourite CDs in my room at night!

6 ....

Do you mean my big black pet spider? My brother says it's horrible, but I think it's lovely!

 B **Put the words into four groups.**

big black blue brown dark fat glass gold high light little
long low metal orange paper pink plastic purple red round
short silver small square tall thin white wood wool yellow

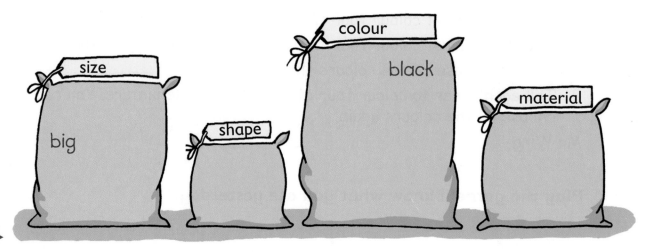

size — big
shape
colour — black
material

C Which words can you use to talk about these?

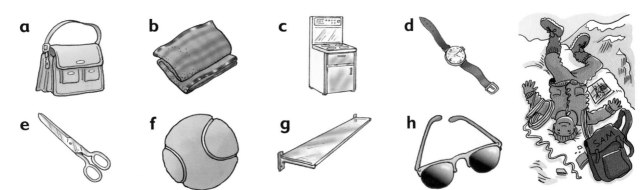

a   b   c   d

e   f   g   h

D   **What did Sally's mum buy in each place? Listen and write a letter in each box.**

Test! Listening Part 3

   e

E Read the story. Choose a word from the box. Write the correct word next to numbers 1–5. There is one example.

Test! Reading & Writing Part 4

Mrs Forest works in the village post office. No one knows if she's 70, 80 or 90, but she's very old. Mrs Forest likes her job. It's always ....busy........ in the post office so she can ask lots of questions. Mrs Forest likes knowing everything about everyone in the village!

Mary Cage from the sweet shop came in to buy six (1) .... 'What was your camping holiday like, Mary?' Mrs Forest asked. 'Did you like sleeping in a (2) .... ?'

Robert Down needed some brown paper. 'Hello, Robert,' Mrs Forest said. 'You (3) .... your motorbike, didn't you? What would you like to buy with all that money?'

Last Saturday it was Mrs Forest's birthday. Her husband, Fred Forest, came into the post office with a big, (4) .... pizza in his hands. 'What's this cheese and pineapple pizza like? Do you know? Would you like this or something else for your birthday (5) .... ? What do you like eating most?' Mr Forest liked asking lots of questions too! 'Chocolate cake!' Mrs Forest answered with a big smile.

Example

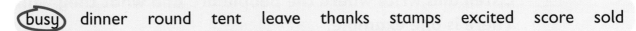

(busy)   dinner   round   tent   leave   thanks   stamps   excited   score   sold

Now choose the best name for the story. Tick one box.

Mrs Forest makes a pizza ☐   Mr and Mrs Forest's questions ☐

Mr Forest's birthday ☐

F Play the game! Guess the adjective.

Where am I?

A Write the places under the pictures.

1 ....

2 ....

3 ....

4 ....

5 ....

6 ....

7 ....

8 ....

B Where do you see these things?

Example

clowns   planes   post box   suitcases   stamps   pilots   taxis
paintings   tents   dinosaurs   envelopes   tickets

horses, ...clowns............
....
....

....
....
....

cards, ...
....
....

....
....
....

 C  **CD1:32** Listen and write where the people are and what they want. There is one example.

Example

In a ....museum........ . The boy wants the girl to ....look at a dinosaur........ .

1 In a .... .The boy wants a .... about ....

2 In a .... .The girl wants ....

 3 In a .... .The class wants to .... more about cars.

Our visit to the factory

Example	Man's name:	David ......Plant......
1	His job:	....
	Two months ago:	Factory began
2		making ....
3	The factory makes:	.... for kitchens
4	You can see:	.... working in the Fast room
5	Time to make one metal part: .... seconds	

 E **Read the text. Choose the right words and write them on the lines.**

Restaurants

Example	People all over ......the...... world love to eat and a lot of people go	a · the · every
1	out .... have a meal in a restaurant. Some people go to restaurants	1 · to · for · from
2	.... their families or friends	2 · by · like · with
3	.... it's their birthday or at Christmas. Some people eat lunch or	3 · what · where · when
4	dinner in restaurants	4 · so · because · and
5	they are away from home or don't .... time to go home and cook.	5 · having · has · have
	There are many different kinds	
6	.... restaurant. You can find	6 · of · on · at
7	.... in big cities and you can	7 · them · it · us
8	.... go and eat in restaurants in the countryside. Some restaurants are very	8 · yet · also · too
9	famous and they might .... expensive. Be careful if you have to pay	9 · were · been · be
10	because you might .... a lot of money!	10 · need · needing · needed

 F **Play the game! Where am I?** 69

They were tired, so ...

A **Answer the questions.**

1 Why do people watch TV?

Different people watch TV at different times of the day. My mum watches the news in the morning to find out about the world and to know what the weather is going to be like. I watch movies and programmes for young people in the afternoon when I come home from school because I'm tired or bored. My dad also watches the news at 9 o'clock. He doesn't have time in the morning!

2 Why do lots of people have computers?

3 Why do people read books?

4 Why do some people go to the circus?

5 Why do people ride bikes?

B **Write so, because or to.**

1 I went to the mountains ...**because**... I love snow sports.

2 Tom can't ski .... he took his sledge.

3 We took our skates with us too .... there was ice on top of the lake.

4 Tom and I picked up some snow .... make a snowman.

5 My hands were cold .... I put on my gloves.

6 I laughed at Tom .... he fell in the snow.

7 Tom was angry with me .... he threw a snowball at me!

8 I put my skis on .... ski down the mountain.

9 I'm going to ski school .... I can learn to ski faster.

C **What things are the same and what things are different?**

D Read the story. Write some words to complete the sentences about the story. You can use 1, 2, 3 or 4 words.

The wrong suitcase!

Lucy and her parents, Mr and Mrs Field, put their summer clothes and swimming things in their big brown suitcase and drove to the airport. Lucy was excited! She loved going on holiday. When the family arrived at the airport, they showed their tickets to a woman in a blue uniform then got on the plane. Lucy's mother read a magazine, her father slept because he was tired and Lucy watched a film. When they got off the plane, it was warm and sunny.

The hotel was ten kilometres away so they took a taxi there. 'Wow!' said Lucy when they arrived. 'Look at that swimming pool! Can we go swimming now?'

'Not yet, Lucy,' her mother said. 'We have to take our things up to our room first.' When Lucy's father picked up the suitcase, he said, 'That's strange. This feels much heavier than it did before!'

Mrs Field laughed. 'You think that because you're tired! Come on! I've got our key. Look! Our room number is 501. It's on the fifth floor.' They went up in the lift, found their room and went inside. Then Lucy's dad opened the suitcase to take out their swimming things.

'Oh no!' he said. 'Whose red hat is this? Why are these big brown shoes in the suitcase? Whose white sweater is this?'

What a terrible mistake! The family had the wrong suitcase!

Examples

The Field family put all their holiday things in a ....big brown suitcase.... .
They went to ....the airport.. by car.

Questions

1 The Field family showed .... to a woman at the airport.

2 When they were on the plane, ... went to sleep.

3 The family went by .... to the hotel because it was a long way away.

4 Lucy wanted to .... when they arrived at the hotel.

5 They went up in the lift because their room was on .... floor.

6 Lucy's father opened the suitcase because he wanted to .... things.

7 Inside the suitcase, they found a red hat, some .... and a white sweater!

E Look at the other pictures. Tell the Paint family's story.

F Play the game! *Why?*

What a strange planet!

 A CD1:34 **Listen! What are Jane and her uncle talking about?**

the sky
wings
spots
trees
fruit
ground
swinging
pocket

 B **Complete the sentences about the picture. Choose the right words and write them on the lines.**

1 The ....biggest.... animals are mice.
2 Horses are smaller .... the other animals.
3 Frogs have got .... longest legs.
4 Monkeys are .... than kangaroos.
5 .... frogs and cows have got wings.
6 .... the animals are awake.

1	bigger	⟨biggest⟩	big
2	than	when	then
3	some	any	the
4	fattest	fat	fatter
5	Any	Both	Lots
6	Every	Another	All

 C CD1:35 **Listen and answer the questions about the competition.**

Which place on our planet would you like to visit?

What's the most beautiful sound that you've ever heard?

Which job is more exciting than an astronaut's job?

What's the best photo that you've ever seen?

 D **Read the text and write the missing words. Write one word on each line.**

That's ⁽¹⁾ ......*an*...... easy question! Every time I turn on the computer, I'm looking ⁽²⁾ .... it! My uncle Jim, who's the best photographer that I know, emailed it ⁽³⁾ .... me. When I saw it, I thought 'Wow!' He took it when he was ⁽⁴⁾ .... holiday. You can see the inside of a cave in it. ⁽⁵⁾ .... are some of the strangest fish in the sea water there. My uncle ⁽⁶⁾ .... a photo competition with it.

 E **Read the letter. Write some words to complete the sentences about the letter. You can use 1, 2, 3 or 4 words.**

Test! Reading & Writing Part 5

Hello, my name's Jack. Last June, I went camping for the first time with Grandpa Peter and with my two cousins who are two years older than I am. It was exciting because we had to put up our tent at night. We couldn't see very much because it was so dark. I didn't know where we were! When I woke up early the next morning, there were so many sounds outside I couldn't believe it! I lay in the tent and listened to the birds that sang all kinds of different songs. I could also hear some water outside, but it sounded louder than a river. I opened the tent quietly because I didn't want to wake my grandfather and cousins. I didn't have any shoes on and the grass under my feet was wet but I didn't mind. This is the most beautiful place that I've ever seen, I thought.

The sound of the water came from a lovely waterfall that was behind some trees – just a little way from the tent. I wish I had a CD now of the music that it made there. I would like to hear it every morning when I wake up!

Examples

Jack and three other people in his family ......*went camping*... last June.
Jack is two years younger than his ......*cousins*...... .

Questions

1 On the first night, Jack could not .... because it was very dark.

2 When Jack woke up, there were lots of .... outside the tent.

3 He listened to the birds and could hear .... outside too.

4 Jack didn't want to wake the other three up, so he .... quietly.

5 Jack enjoyed walking on the .... with no shoes on!

6 Jack found a .... behind the trees.

7 Jack wishes he had a CD of .... that he heard on his camping holiday.

 F **Write yes or no.**

Unit 35 · Having fun

A **Write ten things you can see in the picture.**

Example: ....*a balcony*........

1 .... 5 .... 9 ....

2 .... 6 .... 10 ....

3 .... 7 ....

4 .... 8 ....

B 🔘 CD2:02 **Listen and draw lines. There is one example.** `Test!` `Listening Part 1`

Vicky   Ben   Jim   Tom

Alex   Emma   Sally

Write a sentence for the name that you did not need.

....

....

74

C Sports quiz.

1	For this sport, people stand or sit near water and try to catch something. They might eat it later!	....
2	Teams of five players bounce and throw the ball in this sport. The teams usually wear shorts and T–shirts in different colours.	....
3	People do this sport in winter when there's snow on the mountains. It's important to wear warm clothes!	....
4	You can play this sport inside or outside. You hit a small ball across the top of a table.	....
5	When we do this sport, we use our arms and legs to push our bodies through water.	....
6	In this sport, you hit a very small hard ball across grass. There are usually 18 flags in the place where you play it.	....
7	People do this sport on ice. It looks like dancing sometimes!	....
8	When we play this, we hit the ball in the air with our hands or arms. We don't want the ball to fall on the ground!	....
9	People do this in boats on lakes or in the sea. Sometimes they have races. It's best to do this sport on a windy day!	....
10	People hit a small hard ball and try to score against the other team in this sport. You can play it on grass or on ice.	....

D Listen and write your answers.

E Look and say how the pictures are different.  Speaking Part 1

75

What a funny family!

A Write the correct words on
the green lines and the correct
names on the pink lines.

1 ....William.... looks after the flags on the ship and tidies the ship's kitchen. He's wearing swimming ....shorts.... with red stars on them today.

2 William's grandfather, whose name is .... , loves fishing. He's wearing an old red and white striped T–shirt. One of his legs is .... of wood!

3 William's sister's name is .... She's got a pet parrot and .... wearing shoes!

4 .... is William's grandmother. She does lots of the cooking on the ship. She never stops singing. The whales often come to .... to her.

5 William's father, ... , is busy all day. He counts his money, watches the sea for .... sharks and tells everyone what they must do!

6 William's mother never takes her spotted hat off. She usually sails the ship at night in the .... of the moon. Her name is ....

shorts	air	listen	made	hates
light	shirts	pushes	wished	dangerous

B  **Listen and colour and write and draw.**

Test! Listening Part 5

 C Look and read. Write **yes** or **no.**

Test! Reading & Writing Part 2

Examples Only one person was
swimming in the sea. .....yes.....

The sky was full of clouds. .....no.....

Questions

1 The shell between the two rocks was the bigger one. ....

2 William was wearing swimming shorts with two stripes on them. ....

3 Ann was watching William from the boat when he found the
treasure. ....

4 Half the shoe was under the sand in front of the treasure box. ....

5 The fish were swimming away from William when he opened
the box. ....

6 William had a comb in one of his pockets. ....

7 There was a towel in the boat that had lots of spots on it. ....

 D **What was each person doing when William or Sue took the photo?**

Learner A

> hiding behind a pyramid   holding a puppy   eating some pasta
> picking up shells   climbing a rock   riding a camel

 E **Think hard! How much can you remember?**

John stays in hospital

 A **Look at the picture and read the story.**

Last December it was very cold. It snowed a lot too. One Saturday, John was playing with his sledge on the hill near his house with a group of friends. Suddenly, he fell and broke his leg. His friends ran to tell his mother. An ambulance came and took John to hospital.

Poor John had to stay in hospital. The nurses and the other children there were very friendly. At first he was happy because he didn't have to go to school. He didn't have to do lots of homework and exams like his friends. He didn't have to do any schoolwork! He just listened to CDs and watched his favourite television programmes all day. But then the Christmas holidays started and John was still in hospital. He was bored. He didn't want to watch television or listen to CDs. He wanted to go home. 'I'm unhappy,' he thought.

But then a man came to his room with a bag of presents and a Christmas tree. John saw him on television sometimes. He was a famous sports star called Paul Windows, and he often visited children who were in hospital. He wasn't the only person who came that day. All the students from his class came to visit him too. And two of his teachers brought him the best present – some Maths homework!

B **Write some words to complete the sentences about the story. You can use 1, 2, 3 or 4 words.**  **Test!** Reading & Writing Part 5

Examples It was snowing last ......December...... .

John was on ....the hill....... playing with his sledge.

1 John .... when he fell off his sledge.

2 John went to hospital in ....

3 John liked the nurses and children there because they were

....

4 In hospital, John liked watching TV and .... too.

5 But soon John began to feel .... and wanted to go home.

6 Then someone came to see him who was a .... and gave him some presents.

7 But on the same day, John's teachers came and gave him ....
.... to do!

C **Listen to the story. Draw lines under the differences.**

 D **Read the diary page and write the missing words.**
Write one word on each line.

Test! Reading & Writing Part 7

Friday

Dear diary,

Example I didn't have ....*to*.......... go to school again today because

1 I'm still here in hospital. But I .... making lots of
new friends and the nurses make us all laugh.

2 At about half .... four, the nicest nurse came into

3 my room and turned .... the TV for me because
Harry's Secret started then. I love that programme!

4 Dinner was OK too. We .... fish and chips! And
Mum visited me and brought me a great present. It's the new

5 CD by my favourite group. I listened to it ....
evening.

 E **Listen and write. There is one example.**

Test! Listening Part 2

Don't forget!

Example Take John's ....*art*.......... book
to hospital

Tell him:

1 Class is studying: ....-.
century paintings

2 Read texts on page: ....

3 Artist's name: Paul ....

4 Write answers in: .... book

5 Exam will be on: .... morning

 F **Play the game! Put words together.**

Mary's school holiday

A CD2:06 **What has Mary done? Tick (✔) the boxes.**

B **Read the letter that Mary sent to her family.**

Dear Mum and Dad,

I'm sorry that I haven't written to you earlier, but I'm fine and I'm having a great time with all my friends. I know this is only a short letter, but here are some funny photos for you too! I'm going to buy an envelope in the hotel shop and then send you this letter and these two pictures. Aren't they great?

See you on Saturday. Our plane will arrive at about three o'clock so I'll get my suitcase and I'll see you at about a quarter to four.

Lots of love, Mary

C CD2:07 **Look at Mary's photo. Listen and draw lines.**
There is one example.

Test! Listening Part 1

Harry   Sarah   Kim

Katy   Betty   Alex   Michael

D **Look at the other photo from Mary.**
Which things are different?

 E **Read the postcard and write the missing words.**
Write one word on each line.

Dear Nick,

Example We've already ......been...... here for four days! There

1 .... so many things to see here! We've already

2 visited a museum. .... had gold toys and strange

clothes in it. We've been to the theatre too. I understood

3 the actors because they .... in English. It was

4 about a famous queen .... lived 4,000 years ago.

5 But I have .... go now. We're going to go to a

restaurant that's outside the city for our evening meal.

I'm waving to you!

See you next week at school.

Mary

 F **Make sentences about the things you've done today.**

A   **Write the words to complete the questions.**

1   Have you ever ....eaten........ with ....chopsticks.... ?

2   Have you ever .... in a .... ?

3   Have you ever .... on .... ?

4   Have you ever .... a .... competition?

5   Have you ever .... to .... or New York?

6   Have you ever .... a leg or an .... ?

7   Have you ever .... a famous ....?

B   **Make sentences about your group.**

All of us have   ....

Everyone has   ....

Most of us have   ....

Half of us have   ....

Only a few of us ....

No one has   ....

C Read about skiing. Choose the right words and write them on the lines.

Skiing

Example Have you ever ....been............ skiing? It's an exciting sport but it isn't a

1 new one. There are very old pictures of people .... are skiing

2 in rock drawings inside caves. Some of .... cave paintings are

5,000 years old!

People call Sondre Norheim 'the father of skiing'. In 1870, Sondre used

3 wood to make .... skis. These were the first skis that could

4 .... on soft snow.

5 Sondre wore .... in an important skiing competition which

6 he won. But skiing isn't only a sport. In countries .... there

7 is always lots of snow, skiing is often the best way .... move

from one place to another.

8 About fifty years ago, lots of families started going ....

skiing holidays in the mountains and in about 1980, people started

9 snowboarding too. Many mountain villages already .... ski lifts

10 for skiers to use. Try this sport now .... you can. It's great fun!

Example	be	were	been				
1	what	who	when	**6**	how	why	where
2	these	this	that	**7**	for	of	to
3	some	any	each	**8**	on	at	by
4	turns	turn	turned	**9**	having	has	have
5	it	them	him	**10**	if	or	but

D CD2:08 Look at the mountain picture in Unit 35.
Listen and write yes or no.

1 .... 2 .... 3 .... 4 ....

5 .... 6 .... 7 .... 8 ....

E Let's talk about things we've done!

What has just happened ?

 A **Read Emma's invitation.**
Write words in the boxes below.

Read Pat's invitation.
Write words in the boxes below.

Hi!
Please come to
my party on
Saturday, 12
November at the
Theatre Café. It starts at 5 pm.
Choose between pizza or burgers!
Please wear sports shoes because
we'll play football later!

Love, Emma

To: Betty; Richard; Helen; Fred; Robert; Tom
From: Pat
Subject: My birthday party

Hello everyone!
This year, my party's at my house – 28 Museum
Street. Don't be late! It starts at 4.30 pm on Tuesday,
15 November.
Hot and cold sandwiches first, then Mum's chocolate
cake!
We'll play lots of different games. Wear your funniest
clothes!

Emma's birthday party

Date?	Saturday, 12 November
Time?	
Place?	
What/eat?	
What/wear?	

Pat's birthday party

Date?	Tuesday, 15 November
Time?	
Place?	
What/eat?	
What/wear?	

 B **Jill and Pat are talking about Pat's birthday party. Read the conversation**
and choose the best answer. Write a letter (A–H) for each answer. You
do not need to use all the letters. There is one example.

Test! **Reading &**
Writing Part 3

Jill: It's your birthday today,
isn't it, Pat?

Example   Pat: ......*F*....... .

Jill: Someone told me. Are you
going to have a party?

1   Pat: ....

Jill: Wow! Have you invited
all your friends?

2   Pat: ....

Jill: And what time does it start?

3   Pat: ....

Jill: Oh! Has your mum bought
a lot of food?

A At five, I think. I'm not sure.
B Yes, we've just been to get
some.
C Yes, she was there this
morning.
D Happy birthday!
E Thank you. I will!
F That's right. I'm twelve.
How did you know?
(Example)
G Yes, I am. I'm very excited.
H Only about ten of them.

4 Pat: ....

      Jill: Great. Have a good time!

5 Pat: ....

      Jill: And next time, please invite me too!

C Look at the picture. Find something for each letter of the alphabet.

Examples   **a** ....armchair....   **b** ....bookcase....

D 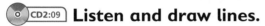 🔊 CD2:09   Listen and draw lines.

 Test! Listening Part 1

Betty   Richard   Helen   Fred

Robert   Tom   Pat

E Read Pat's diary and write the missing words. Write one word on each line.

 Test! Reading & Writing Part 7

> TUESDAY 15 NOVEMBER
>
> **Example**   I was twelve ....*years*.... old today. I got some excellent presents!
>
> **1**   Ten .... my friends came to my party. Tom gave me a computer game about finding bats in a basement! I haven't tried
>
> **2**   to .... it yet, but it looks good. Sally bought me a T–shirt.
>
> **3**   .... 's got an octopus on the front! I got a bike from
>
> **4**   Mum and Dad. Wow! But .... most exciting present was from Uncle David. He's just given me a puppy with lots of white
>
> **5**   fur on its back! I'm going to .... it 'Monster', I think!

F Play the game! Find your partner.

We've moved house!

A **Look at the picture. What are the sentences about? Choose words from the box to complete the sentences.**

1 Pets like .... or birds can live inside this.
  It's often .... of metal.   ....a cage..........

2 These often have photos and stories in them and you
  can buy them in .... where they ....
  newspapers.   ....

3 You don't usually .... to turn this on in the morning,
  but you might want to turn it on when it gets ....

4 You can .... outside through this because it's made of
  .... It's usually square and has wood, metal or plastic
  round it.   ....

> dry   see   made   took   balconies   mice
> glass   shops   dark   sell   fridges   need

B **Look and read. Write yes or no.**

Test! Reading & Writing Part 2

Examples

There are some magazines on the table that's square.   ...yes...
The animal that's inside the cage is holding out its wings.   ...no...

Questions

1 You can only see three people in this living room.   ....

2 Someone has already opened the box that's under the window.   ....

3 Both the men who are carrying the sofa have blond moustaches.   ....

4 You can see a picture of a dog under the light.   ....

5 The pet with the striped tail is lying down.   ....

6 Someone has turned on the lamp that's got spots on it.   ....

7 The woman's just picked up the plant that's in the corner of the room.   ....

 C (CD2:10) **Where has Katy's mum put Katy's things?**
Listen and write a letter in each box. There is one example.

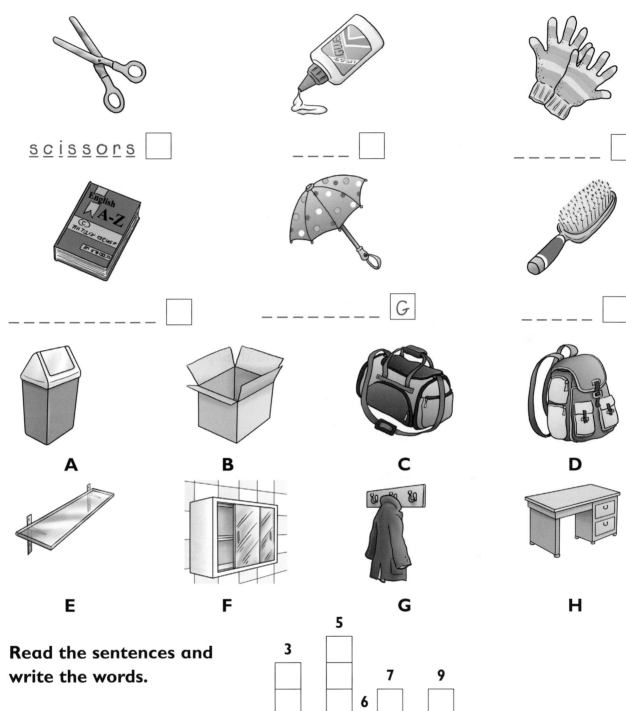

s c i s s o r s [ ]

_ _ _ _ [ ]

_ _ _ _ _ _ [ ]

English A-Z

_ _ _ _ _ _ _ _ _ _ [ ]

_ _ _ _ _ _ _ _ [G]

_ _ _ _ _ _ [ ]

A   **B**   **C**   **D**

E   **F**   **G**   **H**

 D **Read the sentences and write the words.**

When do these things happen?

A **Read the questions and write words in the boxes.**

January ☐	.... ☐	March ☐	.... ☐
May ☐	June ☐	.... ☐	.... ☐
September ☐	October ☐	November ☐	.... ☐

1 Write the missing months on the lines.

2 How many days are there in each month? Write the answer in each small box.

3 Write today's date in the correct box.

4 What date is your birthday?

5 Colour the summer months yellow and the spring months light green. Choose two more colours to show the winter and autumn months too.

6 Draw a star in your favourite month.

B 🔘 CD2:11 **Listen and tick (✔) the box. There is one example.** Test! Listening Part 4

Which place did Richard and his class visit?

A ☐   B ☐   C ✔

1 When did Richard's school holiday begin?

APRIL 29   JUNE 4   SEPTEMBER 18

A ☐   B ☐   C ☐

2 What did Richard do on holiday?

A ☐   B ☐   C ☐

3 What did Richard bring home?

A ☐   B ☐   C ☐

4 When can Richard's aunt watch the holiday film?

A ☐   B ☐   C ☐

5 What will Richard wear?

A ☐   B ☐   C ☐

C Put the words in the right place.

five o'clock summer
Tuesday 6 am August 9 pm
February half past ten
midnight 2003 midday
Wednesday morning
quarter to three July
Friday evening Thursday
Christmas autumn
the weekend spring

in	on	at
....	....	*five o'clock*
....	....	....
....	....	....
....	....	....
....	....	....
....	....	....
....	....	....
....	....	....
....	....	....

D Use the words from C to complete the questions.

1 What were you doing at .... ?

2 What did you do at .... ?

3 Are you going to study on .... ?

4 Were you in bed at .... ?

5 Where were you in .... ?

6 Where will you be at .... ?

E Read the text. Choose the right words and write them on the lines.

Example Our planet takes 365 and a quarter days to .....*move*..... round the sun, so every four years we have a 'leap'

1 year. In a leap year, ... are 366 days so we add another day to the month of February. Twelve

2 months .... one year. Most

3 months have 31 days, but four .... the months in a year only have 30 days. February is

4 the month .... only has 28 or 29 days.

5 Twice a year, ... countries in the world decide to change the time by one hour. We do

6 this .... we want to use more light from the sun. It's easier for people who work outside if we change the time. It's better for people that

7 have to do .... lot of driving too. We

8 change the time .... the end of March and October. In March, we make the time one hour later and in October, one hour earlier. So,

9 on the first day after the clocks ....

10 changed in October, ... can stay in bed for another hour! Excellent!

	move	moved	moving
1	there	those	they
2	make	makes	making
3	of	from	with
4	who	which	what
5	many	much	lots
6	because	than	but
7	the	a	any
8	on	past	at
9	have	has	having
10	he	you	it

Test! Reading & Writing Part 6

89

I might be a famous sports star!

A 🔘 CD2:12 What might Sam be one day?

1 Sam won't be a ....dentist.......... because that's a ....boring.......... job.

2 Sam might be an .... but that's a .... job.

3 Sam may be a .... because that's an .... job.

4 Sam says he'll be a .... That's a .... job!

B What are they thinking?

I .... be a
....

I .... be a
....

I .... be a
....

I .... be a
....

C Choose your answers. Tick (✔) the boxes.

In ten years …

1 I'll be
- ☐ at school.
- ☐ at university.
- ☐ at work.

2 I'll live
- ☐ here.
- ☐ in another city.
- ☐ in another country.
- ☐ on another planet.

3 I won't have
- ☐ any homework.
- ☐ any friends.
- ☐ any money.
- ☐ any problems.

4 I'll be
- ☐ single.
- ☐ married.

5 I may have
- ☐ a castle.
- ☐ a motorbike.
- ☐ a swimming pool.
- ☐ a horse.
- ☐ an island.
- ☐ a piano.

6 I might be
- ☐ a businessman/woman.
- ☐ a doctor.
- ☐ an engineer.
- ☐ a nurse.
- ☐ a farmer.
- ☐ a famous sports star!

D CD2:13 **What did Mrs Kind give to each of her friends?**
Listen and write a letter in each box. There is one example.

Katy [C]   Richard ☐   Emma ☐

Michael ☐   Sarah ☐   Robert ☐

A   B   C   D

E   F   G   H

E **Answer me!**

Yes, I will.

I may!

I might.

No, I won't!

1 Will you remember all the new words on these two pages? ....

2 Will you phone your best friend this evening? ....

3 Will you have a party on your next birthday? ....

4 Will you be a famous tennis player one day? ....

F **Our predictions.**

 A **Write each of the words under *him*, *her* or *both*. There is one example.**

	him	her	both
	he		

he wife son sister
grown-up husband people
Miss grandpa aunt cousin
child grandfather Mr queen
person Mrs grandma
grandson uncle
granddaughter parent
baby king them

 B  **Listen and write. There is one example.** *Test!* Listening Part 2

	John Silkwood visits our town		
Example	Name of son:	Michael	
1	Son lives in	.... Street	
2	John has	.... grandsons	
3	Started singing lessons when he was	.... years old	
4	Enjoys playing the	.... most	
5	Name of favourite song:	....	

 C **Read the text. Choose a word from the box. Write the correct word next to numbers 1–5. There is one example.** *Test!* Reading & Writing Part 4

Hello! My name's Sarah but many of you may think I'm ....called....... Sue Pepper. That's just the name I use for my work. I'm 21. I'm an actor and I love horse–riding in my free time. I've already been in lots of (1) .... , but now I'm working with my best friend, Mary, on a new TV programme. It's very funny and you can see it soon! I can't tell you the name of the programme because that's a (2) .... Sorry! The place where we are filming is a long way from my house so I fly there in a helicopter each day. I feel very (3) .... ! I have to wear all kinds of strange clothes and do all kinds of dangerous things like going for a (4) .... with a tiger or jumping off a high rock into a (5) .... I got very wet that day! But I mustn't tell you any more. Bye for now.

Example

called   secret   terrible   taste   future   famous   walk   waterfall   movies   teach

Now choose the best name for this text. Tick one box.

Sarah, the actor ☐   Sarah, the helicopter pilot ☐   Sarah's secret place ☐

D **Read the text again and write 1, 2 or 3 words in each box.**

Test! Speaking Part 2

Sarah	Age?	Works with?	Job?	Goes to work by?	Hobby?
	21				

E **Ask your teacher questions about Richard and write words in the boxes below.**

Test! Speaking Part 2

Age?	
Works with?	
Job?	
Goes to work by?	
Hobby?	

F **Draw, write, then talk about a person you know.**

Age?	
Works with?	
Job?	
Goes to work by?	
Hobby?	

Unit 45

A ⊙ CD2:15 **Listen and write. There is one example.**

Test! Listening Part 2

Example	Name: Richard .....Hudson.....
1	Job: ....
2	Makes things with: wood and ....
3	Starts work at: ....
4	Works in: the ....
5	Making now: ....

B **Ask and answer questions about Tony, Vicky, Alex and Kim.**

C **Read the text. Choose a word from the box.**
Write the correct word next to numbers 1–5.

You can see many different kinds of interesting people on David Sun's TV
(1) .....programme..... . Every Thursday evening, thousands of people in
(2) .... , towns and villages (3) .... on their televisions to watch
him. Each week, David talks to different singers, music groups, artists,
(4) .... business people and other exciting people. Tonight, David Sun is
going to talk to one of the most beautiful (5) .... stars, Helen Keys!

> high countries lie famous
> programme film cities turn idea

D **Now read the text and write David Sun's questions.**

Example **David:** .....G.....

Helen: Hello, everyone! Hello, David!
It's great to see you again.

1 David:

....

Helen: Yes. I got here at midday.

2 David: ....

   Helen: To make a new film with my husband.

3 David: ....

   Helen: The life of a famous painter.

4 David: ....

   Helen: Just for one week. We are going to film a new movie in the jungle next month.

5 David: ....

   Helen: Next spring.

A Why have you come to London?

B How long will you be here?

C Have you just arrived?

D When will your film be in the cinemas?

E What's the film about?

F Who are you going to visit now?

G Now let's meet the lovely Helen Keys! (**Example**)

H Me too! I love doing that!

 E **Read Sam's email to David Sun.**

Hi David,

I went to the World Zoo today. Someone told me about the new dolphin trainer who works there. His name's Alex Sugar. He's not famous like other people on your programme, but he's very interesting and funny and so are the dolphins at the zoo! But there's a problem. Alex Sugar can come to the film studio, but the dolphins can't. So we'll have to take all our cameras and lights to the zoo and film him, the dolphins and the programme there. Do you agree?

Sam

 F **Look at the pictures. Tell the story.**

Here's my news!

A **Look at the pictures. Which parts of Low Island School can you see?**

a  **b**  **c**  **d**  **e**  **f**

the office   ....

....

the sports hall   the library   the computer room

(the office)   the playground   the dining room

B **CD2:16 Listen to Nick. Which part of the school is he in?**

Example ....d....   **3** ....

1 ....   **4** ....

2 ....

C **Ask and answer about Helen and Robert's hotels.**

Test! Speaking Part 2

Learner A
Helen Kite's hotel

Learner B
Robert Brown's hotel

Where/hotel?	on Dolphin Island
How many rooms?	27
What/can do?	swimming or water-skiing
Where/room?	1st floor
What/see from the window?	coconut trees

Where/hotel?	next to City Airport
How many rooms?	610
What/can do?	golf or dancing
Where/room?	11th floor
What/see from the window?	car factory

D Read the sentences in boxes 1–5. Who wrote each of them, Anna or Fred?

Anna is in Britain. She's studying English. Fred is at the beach.

Text 1

Dear Ben,

Here is a postcard of the school where I'm studying English.

Anna

Text 2

Dear Ben,

Here is a postcard of the beach which is near our hotel.

Fred

1	a	We've been at this hotel since Monday.
	b	My teachers are nice, but my English is terrible!
2	a	There's a park near the school where I go with the other students.
	b	Tonight we're going to have dinner in a café which is opposite the beach.
3	a	I've made lots of friends with the other children who are staying at the hotel.
	b	I've made lots of friends but one boy is very naughty.
4	a	The grown-ups sit in the sun and we play in the water.
	b	Yesterday he tried to burn the papers in the classroom bin!
5	a	After school, we can choose between sport, watching DVDs or playing on the computer.
	b	We meet at the swimming pool after lunch.

E CD2:17 Listen to Paul. He's talking about his day.

F Write about <u>your</u> school or news.

Unit 47 Let's have some fun!

 A **Follow the lines to make suggestions.**

Would you like   phoning for two pizzas?

Why don't we   playing my new computer game?

Let's   watch my favourite DVD.

What about   to go shopping with me?

Shall we   buy those pink sweets?

How about   meet next to the bridge?

B **Read the conversation and choose the best answer.**
Write a letter (A–H) for each answer. There is one example.

> **Test!** Reading & Writing Part 3

Example

 Michael: Hello! Is that you, Richard?

 Richard: ....B......

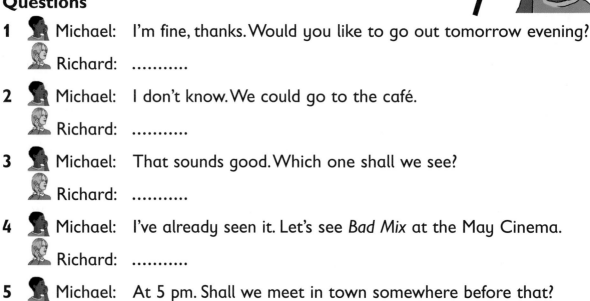

Questions

1   Michael: I'm fine, thanks. Would you like to go out tomorrow evening?

     Richard: ....

2   Michael: I don't know. We could go to the café.

     Richard: ....

3   Michael: That sounds good. Which one shall we see?

     Richard: ....

4   Michael: I've already seen it. Let's see *Bad Mix* at the May Cinema.

     Richard: ....

5   Michael: At 5 pm. Shall we meet in town somewhere before that?

     Richard: ....

A OK! I'll see you at the bus stop at 4.30!

B Yes, it's me. How are you? (**Example**)

C All right. What time does it start?

D Good idea, but what would you like to do?

E Did you? I bought two DVDs from there.

F *Monster Castle?* It's a funny one, I think.

G The actress is called Tiger Try.

H I don't like it there. What about going to see a film?

C **What's happening in the theatre? Look and write yes or no.**

1 The man who's wearing a sweater has a piece of paper in his left hand. ....yes....

2 The girl who's flying with orange wings has got short dark hair.   ....

3 Someone is sitting on the chair that is by the book.   ....

4 You can see a flag with a star on it at the back of the boat.   ....

5 A person who's carrying an envelope is going up the stairs.   ....

   Listen and colour and draw and write.

D

E **Shall we write a story?**

Bill and Helen's mother is an actress and she had to work at the theatre on Friday. Bill and Helen were bored at home. They looked out of the window. They looked through their CDs and DVDs, but they were still bored. They decided to go upstairs to their bedrooms. When their mother came home from work, she was very happy.

It's too loud!

A Read and say why.

1 Look at these words. What do they start with? Why?

Yes.	Betty	Miss Black	London	Tuesday	August	English
No.						

Write another example of each kind of word in the empty boxes.

2 What's at the end of each of the sentences in **a** and **b**?

   a Are you ready? What time does your plane leave? Sorry? That's your cousin Paul, isn't it?

   b Yes. That's right. I had a great time today.

3 Why is there an apostrophe (') in these sentences?

   You shouldn't do that.   Jill's gone home.

   Jane's a very good singer.   John's dog is very naughty.

B Write the sentence then choose another sentence to follow it.

1 thelorrycantgounderthatbridge
   The lorry can't go under that bridge.
   It's too low.

2 canyouturnthemusicdownplease
   ....
   ....

3 icouldntdomymathshomeworklastnight
   ....
   ....

4 inwinterwecantplayfootballafterfiveoclock
   ....
   ....

5 whydidntyougotoemmasparty
   ....
   ....

6 itsnotgoingtosnowtoday
   ....
   ....

It's not cold enough.   Because it's too dark.   I was too tired.
It's too loud.   ~~It's too low.~~   I didn't have enough time.

C Answer these questions. Use *too* or *enough* in your answers.

1 Why don't you live in the jungle?

Because I'm not brave enough. It's too dangerous.

2 Why can't you pick up a giraffe?

....

3 Why do you need to turn on the light at night?

....

4 Why can't you climb Mount Everest?

....

5 Why don't you drive a car?

....

D Listen, then write the missing words.

Mum: Wake up, wake up!

It's time to go (1) ....to........ school!

John: I'm tired. (2).............. back hurts.

I want to stay (3).............. bed.

Mum: No, John, no!

You must (4).............. up now, it's late!

John: It's not. It's too early. I'm not going (5)..............!

I'm not going anywhere!

(6)..............'s a storm outside.

It's raining (7).............. hard and it's too cold.

Mum: No, John, no!

It's sunny (8).............. warm.

You're (9).............. holiday.

You were having (10).............. bad dream!

E Look at these two pictures. Which things are different?

F Play the game! Guess my four things.

If I feel bored

A CD2:20 **Listen and say which picture. Then listen and say how picture 3 is different.**

1

3

B **Read the story. Choose a word from the box. Write the correct word next to numbers 1–5. There is one example.**

Test! Reading & Writing Part 4

Helen and her father often go to the park together ....*early*........ in the morning before Helen goes to school. Her father wants to run in a long (1) .... this summer so he needs to practise. He tries to run five kilometres every morning. Helen doesn't run with him. She (2) .... to skip. She's excellent at it. She can skip faster than all the other girls in her class. But last Monday, Helen's dad (3) .... into some water. He felt very cold after that and had to go home and lie down on the sofa under a (4) ....

'I'm not going to go for a run tomorrow, Helen,' he said. 'Perhaps you should stay at home too.' Helen felt unhappy when her dad said that. Skipping in the park makes her feel happy all day. Helen's dad saw that Helen was sad. 'It will only be for one day!' he said. 'We can go running and skipping again on Wednesday!'

Helen felt much (5) .... after that!

Example

| early | better | grew | race | pushes |
| blanket | dangerous | prefers | fell | problem |

Now choose the best name for the story.

Tick one box.

Helen's dad learns to skip ☐   Helen's dad buys a new blanket ☐

Helen's dad gets wet ☐

C **Draw lines between the two halves of the sentences.**

1 When I'm unhappy about something and want to talk
2 If I'm feeling thirsty and need a drink
3 When I'm feeling very happy
4 If I'm feeling hot, I open a window or
5 When I'm ill, my mum brings me a spoon and

a I smile and sing loudly.
b I phone my best friend.
c I get some water.
d I take my medicine.
e I turn on the fan.

 D **Finish these sentences.**

1 When I'm tired, _I close my eyes and try to sleep for a few minutes._
2 I laugh when ....
3 I cry if ....
4 Sometimes I feel afraid when ....
5 If I'm bored, I usually ....
6 .... make(s) me angry.

 E **Complete the sentences about picture 1 in A.**

Mr (1) .... and his daughter Helen went to the park. Before they left home, Mr (1) .... put on a (2) .... and some (3) ....

He took his sports shoes out of (4) .... Before Helen left home with her father, she put on her clean (5) ....

 F **Tell the story.**

2

4

 G **Play the game! Which word?**

Vicky   Sally   David   Lucy

Nick   Jane   Jack

B **Find the second half of each sentence and write it on the line.**

1 The girl with long straight hair is using glue ..*to make a rocket.*...................................

2 The woman is cutting some bread because ....
....

3 The biggest boy is cutting a newspaper into pieces because ....
....

4 The girl with the hat is trying ....
....

5 Two girls in warm clothes are enjoying ....
....

to do her homework at the kitchen table.

she's going to make more sandwiches.

making a snowman in the garden.

he's helping to make a rocket.

~~to make a rocket.~~

C   **Read and complete the sentences with the correct form of _make_ or _do_.**

My mum's a doctor and she's got to work at the hospital this morning
so my brother, my three sisters and I are all going to help her. I'm going
to ....*do*............ some shopping. David is going to (1) ....
pizzas for all of us for lunch because he loves cooking. Lucy is going to
help our youngest sister, Jane, to learn all her spellings. Jane's got to
(2) .... a test on Monday morning and she hates (3) ....
mistakes!

Sally and David are going to (4) ....
everyone's bed. There's lots of work for all of us to
(5) .... !
But tomorrow is Sunday so that will be a fun day!
All the family go to the sports centre and
(6) .... all kinds of different sports there.
My favourite sport is hockey. What's yours?

Vicky

 D   **Now let's talk about you and the things you do.**
   Complete, then ask and answer the questions.

   1   Who ....*makes*............ the breakfast in your house?

   ....

   2   Who .... your bed?

   ....

   3   What subjects do you .... at school?

   ....

   4   Where do you .... your homework?

   ....

   5   Tell me about the sports you .... and the sports you like to watch.

   ....

E   **Play the game! Sit on the right chair.**

 105

What a lot of questions!

A **Which words do you need in these questions?**

What kind   How long   What   ~~Who~~
Have you ever   How   Can   Are you   Whose

Questions	Tom	Me	....
1 .... ~~Who~~ .... is your favourite actor?	....	....	....
2 .... in any clubs?	....	....	....
3 .... have you been in this class?	....	....	....
4 .... is your favourite English word?	....	....	....
5 .... you play the piano?	....	....	....
6 .... written a song?	....	....	....
7 .... of music do you like?	....	....	....
8 .... house did you visit last week?	....	....	....
9 .... tall are you?	....	....	....

B  CD2:22 **Listen to the questions and write Tom's answers.**

C **Read the story. Write some words to complete the sentences about the story. You can use 1, 2, 3 or 4 words.**

SARAH 136   HARRY 142

Harry and the difficult questions

Harry Doors loved learning. He had hundreds of books in his room at home and liked using the computer at school to find out about jungles, clouds, kangaroos or anything else that he found interesting.

One day Harry's teacher said, 'Would you like to be on a TV programme, Harry? It's a competition for the cleverest children in the country. You'll have to answer lots of difficult questions!' Harry said, 'Yes! Of course!'

The next day, a man called Mr Silver came to Harry's school to talk to him about the competition. 'Before we can film you, Harry,' he said, 'I have three quick questions for you. Ready?' 'Yes!' Harry whispered. He was a little afraid!

'Good! Where's the River Thames?' 'In London,' Harry said quietly.

'Well done! What's 27 times 5?' '135!' Harry answered quickly.

'Great! Which is the highest mountain in the world?' 'Mount Everest and it's 8,848 metres high!' Harry answered with a big smile on his face. He knew that all his answers were right.

'Excellent!' the man said. 'You're clever enough for the competition next Tuesday. A taxi will bring you and your parents to Television House at six o'clock! Now, I just need to know your age. When's your birthday, Harry?' Harry was so excited he couldn't speak. 'Sorry!' he said. 'I've forgotten!'

Examples

.... *Doors* .... was Harry's surname.

In Harry's room at home there were .... *hundreds of books* ....

Questions

1 Harry used .... to find out lots of things.

2 The first person to tell Harry about the .... on TV was his teacher.

3 The .... in Harry's country will be on the TV programme.

4 The name of the man who came to see Harry was ....

5 The man wanted to ask Harry three ....

6 Harry was happy because .... were right.

7 But Harry couldn't remember the date of his .... !

D  **Listen and colour.**

Give me a short answer!

A CD2:24 **Who's talking? Match the numbers and letters.**

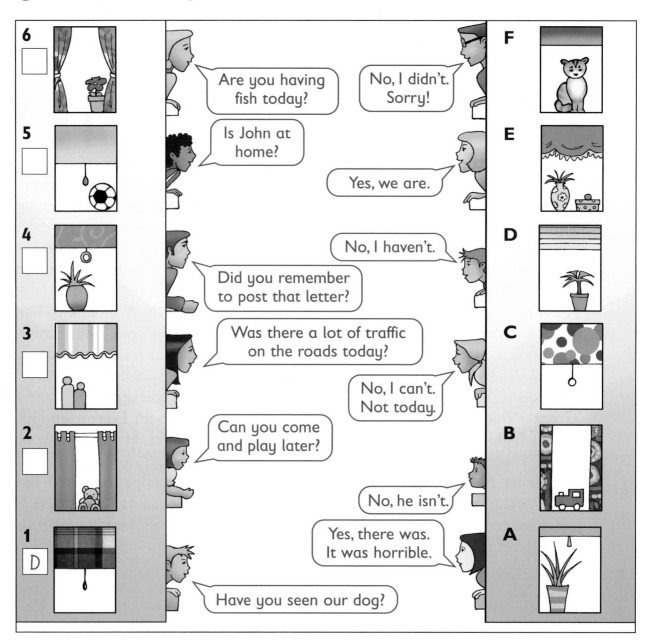

Are you having fish today?

No, I didn't. Sorry!

Is John at home?

Yes, we are.

No, I haven't.

Did you remember to post that letter?

Was there a lot of traffic on the roads today?

No, I can't. Not today.

Can you come and play later?

No, he isn't.

Yes, there was. It was horrible.

Have you seen our dog?

6

5

4

3

2

1 | D |

F

E

D

C

B

A

B **Write your answers.**

Learner A

1 Have you got a pet at home? .... , I ....

2 Did you go to the cinema last month? .... , I ....

3 Are your shoes black? .... , they ....

4 Do you and your friends see each other every day? .... , we ....

5 Do shops sell things? .... , they ....

Learner B

1　Was it sunny yesterday afternoon?　　　.............. , it ....

2　Did you watch TV last night?　　　.............. , we ....

3　Did you come to school by bus today?　　　.............. , I ....

4　Do you look like anyone in your family?　　　.............. , I ....

5　Would you like to stop writing now?　　　.............. , I ....

C　**Look at the picture and read the story. Write some words to complete the sentences about the story. You can use 1, 2, 3 or 4 words.**

Naughty Daisy

Last Sunday, our family wanted to go and see the new animals that have arrived at our town zoo. But when we got up that morning, the weather was very cold and windy so it wasn't a good day to be outside. We decided to stay at home.

After lunch, my little sister Daisy was bored, so she came into my bedroom and asked, 'Tony, can you play this board game with me?' 'Sorry, Daisy,' I said, 'I can't. I have to study for my Science exam. I'll play with you later.'

Then Daisy went to the living room. Dad was there. 'Would you like to play with me, Dad?' she asked. 'Yes, I would, Daisy, but I'm busy now,' he answered. 'I'll play with you in ten minutes. I must finish this long and important letter first.'

Mum was in the hall. Daisy started to ask her to play with her too, but Mum said, 'Wait, Daisy. I'm talking to Aunt Sarah on the phone.'

'I can't find anyone to play with,' thought Daisy. She felt angry. She went upstairs to fetch her dolls.

When Dad finished his work, he called Daisy's name. Then Mum finished speaking to Aunt Sarah and called her name too. Daisy didn't answer. I stopped reading and listened and went downstairs because I heard her laugh. 'She's in the kitchen,' I thought. 'Why is she in there?'

Example

The family didn't go out on Sunday because it was ...~~very cold and windy~~.. outside.

1　........................... was studying for his Science exam.

2　Daisy's father had to write his .... in the living room.

3　Daisy's mother couldn't talk to Daisy. She was speaking to ....

4　Daisy was .... because no one could play with her.

5　Daisy didn't answer when her .... called her name.

6　Tony heard Daisy laugh so he went ....

7　Tony wanted to know why Daisy was in ....

D　**Play the game! Put your hand on it first.**

A Read the text. Choose the right words and write them on the lines.

 Test! Reading & Writing Part 6

WATER AND RIVERS

Example	Water is very important on our planet and ....we........ all need it to live. People and animals		we it he
1	drink it. Farmers use it to grow food	**1**	to from for
2	people to eat. Fish and .... sea animals	**2**	others another other
	live in it. The water on our planet isn't the same		
3	.... The water in the sea has salt in it.	**3**	everything everyone everywhere
	You can taste this if you go swimming in it. But the		
	water in rivers hasn't got any salt in it. And water		
4	is .... always the same temperature.	**4**	no not nowhere
5	In some places, it's so cold that we	**5**	seen sees see
6	ice on the top of water. But .... the	**6**	than if so
	weather is warmer, this never happens. But where		
7	.... water come from? Water can come	**7**	does do done
8	from rivers or through rocks .... are	**8**	that who what
	under the ground. It can also come from the sky		
	in rain or snow. Rivers are very important to		
9	.... We use rivers to take things from	**9**	them us it
10	one place to another .... boat. Villages,	**10**	with like by
	towns and cities are often next to rivers because		
	people can use the water to drink and grow their		
	food.		

B Complete the sentences about water. Use 1, 2, 3 or 4 words.

1 In ....the sea........ , water has salt in it.

2 There is .... of water in some very cold places.

3 Water falls .... when it rains or snows.

4 Some people .... up and down rivers by boat.

5 People don't only .... water, they also use it to grow food.

C **Listen and write. There is one example.**

The River Thames

Example	Name of river:	The .... <u>*Thames*</u>
1	How long:	.... kilometres
2	Person who lives in the castle:	the ....
3	How many kinds of fish:	....
4	People's hobbies here:	fishing and ....
5	Colour of *Sister Susie*:	.... and blue

D **Ask and answer about world rivers.**

E **Listen to the story. Write 1, 2, 3 or 4 next to the pictures.**

It was David's birthday last week. His parents gave him a very exciting and expensive present: some water-skiing classes! Today he's having his first lesson!

a ☐

b ☐

c ☐

d 1

 A **Find the places on the map. Then read the sentences and write the other places.**

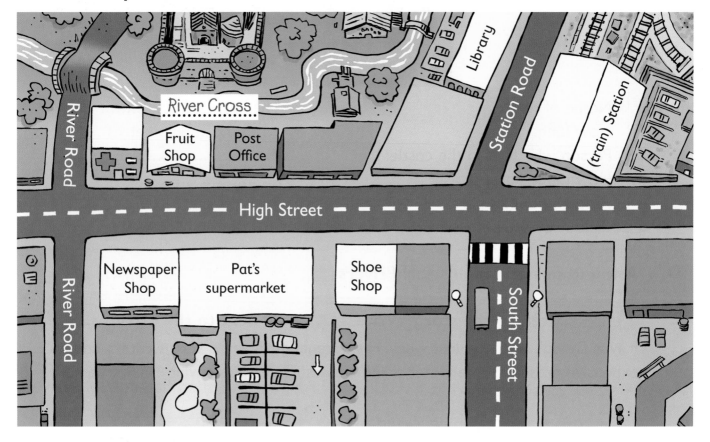

1   The river near this town is called the River Cross. It starts in the hills, runs down past our town and then it becomes part of the River West.

2   There's a bank on the corner of South Street and High Street, opposite the train station.

3   The post office is on High Street. It's across the street from the supermarket which opened last month.

4   A new sports shop has just opened. It's on River Road near the newspaper shop. All their hockey shirts are very cheap this week if you need a new one.

5   If you need to buy some medicine, there's a very friendly chemist's on the corner of River Road. It's very easy to see because it has a green cross outside.

6   There isn't a bus station in this town, but you can wait for the bus at the bus stops on both sides of South Street. The 11 o'clock bus has just stopped there.

7   If you need somewhere to stay, there's an excellent hotel across the street from the train station. It's called the Station Hotel because it's on the road with the same name.

8   A new restaurant is going to open between the hotel and the post office. The name outside says The Food Village so I think they're going to sell different kinds of food.

B **Listen and tick (✔) the box. There is one example.**

What can Richard buy?

A ☐   B ✔   C ☐

1 Which place is opposite the library now?

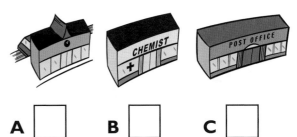

A ☐   B ☐   C ☐

2 How will Richard and his parents get to the castle?

3 Which train will Richard's family get?

A ☐   B ☐   C ☐   A ☐   B ☐   C ☐

4 What will Richard have for dinner in the restaurant?

5 What did Richard lose in the city?

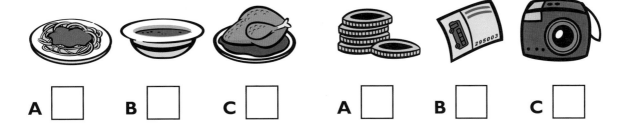

A ☐   B ☐   C ☐   A ☐   B ☐   C ☐

 C **Ask and answer questions.**  Test! Speaking Part 4

Learner A

Now let's talk about shopping.
Which shops do you usually buy your clothes in?
How often do you buy sweets or chocolate?
Have you ever bought something on the Internet?
Which shops don't you like?
Tell me about your favourite shop.

 D **Be actors in a shop or town!**

Fun and games!

A

We had so much fun! Listen and draw lines.

Test! Listening Part 1

Robert   Lucy   Michael

Have a   holiday!

Katy   Betty   Helen   William

B   **We're having a party! Invite your best friend.**

....

....

....

....

....

....

....

114

C **Robert's favourite word game.**

green	autumn	coat	swim	bus
belt	camel	ski	kangaroo	minutes
red	puppy	engineer	draw	tomorrow
above	surprised	fire engine	purple	missing
taxi	black	angry	singer	footballer
near	shorts	moustache	below	ambulance
monster	midnight	Tuesday	gloves	hungry
artist	maths	afraid	white	monkey
hide	over	waiter	ring	museum
truck	excited	kitten	dance	opposite

Unit 5 — My things

Learner A

Read and answer these questions.

1 What do you carry your school things in? ....

2 What presents did you get for your last birthday? ....

3 What's on the table beside your bed? ....

4 What things do you usually put in your pockets? ....

Unit 8 — School subjects

Learner A

Ask your friend these questions about school.

	Lesson 1		Lesson 2	Lesson 3		Lesson 4	Lesson 5
Monday		B			L		
Tuesday		R			U		
Wednesday		E			N		
Thursday		A			C		
Friday		K			H		

1 What's your favourite subject? ....

2 How many hours of English do you study every week? ....

3 What subjects have you got on Monday morning? ....

4 Who teaches you Maths? ....

5 Which teacher gives you the most homework? ....

6 Which subjects do you think are interesting? ....

7 When's your next exam? ....

8 Which sports are you learning to play at school? ....

What they eat

Learner A

Ask and answer questions.

May's pet

What kind/animal?	....
Like/eating?	....
Colour/pet?	....
Age?	....
Name/pet?	....

Unit 22

The time of the year

Learner A

Ask your friend these questions and write their answers.

What time of the year do you usually go on holiday?   ....

What's your favourite day of the week?   ....

What's your favourite month of the year?   ....

Which month is usually the hottest where you live?   ....

Where do you usually go at the weekend?   ....

Which century would you most like to live in?   ....

My things

Learner B

**Read and answer
these questions.**

1 What's on your bedroom walls? ....

2 What did you buy the last time you went shopping? ....

3 What things is it important to take on holiday? ....

4 Are you a tidy or untidy person? ....

School subjects

Learner B

Ask your friend these questions about school.

	Lesson 1		Lesson 2	Lesson 3		Lesson 4	Lesson 5
Monday		B			L		
Tuesday		R			U		
Wednesday		E			N		
Thursday		A			C		
Friday		K			H		

1 How many students are there in your class? ....

2 What's your favourite school day? ....

3 Are you good at Art? ....

4 How many different teachers have you got? ....

5 Where do you usually do your homework? ....

6 How many books do you have for Geography? ....

7 What subjects have you got on Thursday afternoon? ....

8 Which subjects do you think are easy? ....

What they eat

Learner B

Ask and answer questions.

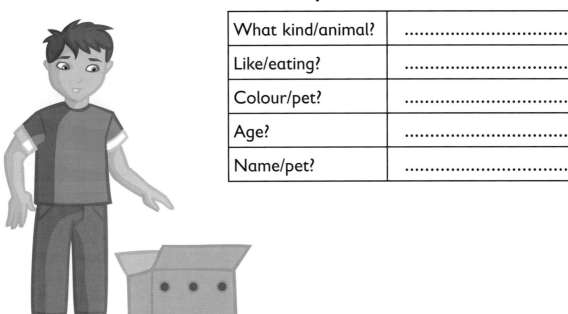

William's pet

What kind/animal?	....
Like/eating?	....
Colour/pet?	....
Age?	....
Name/pet?	....

The time of the year

Learner B

Ask your friend these questions and write their answers.

When's your birthday? ....

Does it often rain where you live? ....

What's your favourite time of the day? ....

Which do you prefer: winter or summer? Why? ....

What do people write in diaries? ....

Do you prefer to tell the time with a phone,
a clock or a watch? ....

Unit 24

Leaving and arriving

Learner A

Ask your friend these questions and write their answers.

1 How do you go to school? ....

2 How long does it take you to get to school? ....

3 Have you ever been in a helicopter? ....

4 What's your favourite kind of car? ....

5 What's the best way to travel on holiday? ....

Unit 32

Where am I?

Learner A

What are these places?

1 You should go to this place if you need to study or read a book.

....

2 People go here when they need to fly for work or holidays.

....

3 When you want to post a letter, you can buy stamps at this place.

....

4 This is a place where people go to study and learn.

....

5 You find these in most towns and people stay in them when they are away from home.

....

What a funny family!

Learner B

What was each person doing when William or Sue took the photo?

hiding behind a pyramid   holding a puppy   eating some pasta
picking up shells   climbing a rock   riding a camel

Unit 44

About people

1 .... is the word for the person that your uncle is married to.

2 If your aunt and uncle have children, these will be your ....

3 In a lot of countries, people believe you are a .... when you are eighteen years old.

4 You can use just one word, ... , to mean 'mother and father'.

5 The person that a husband is married to is his ....

6 If your son has a daughter, then she's your ....

7 When you write or talk to a man and you only know his surname, you can say .... before his surname.

Unit 24

Learner B

Ask your friend these questions and write their answers.

1 Do you usually arrive early or late for school? ....

2 When was the last time you travelled in a taxi? ....

3 Are you afraid of flying? ....

4 Would you like to visit the moon? ....

5 Can you name a famous driver? ....

Unit 32 Where am I?

Learner B

What are these places?

1 We must wait at this place before we get on a train.

2 This place is outside and it may have a lot of swings and other games for children.

....

3 You go to this place if you want to see tigers and clowns.

....

4 People make things here like cars, fridges and computers, for example.

....

5 At this place, we can learn about things from different places and times.

....

122

Unit 54

Finding your way

Learner B

Now let's talk about places you go to.

What's your favourite place to go at weekends?

Which cinema do you usually go to? Where is it?

Where can you go to do sport in your town?

Are there any new shops in your town?

Tell me about the shops in one of the streets where you live.

Unit 13

Food and drink

25–30

Well done! You eat very well and you look after your body. This is important because at your age you are growing.

15–24

Come on! Some of the things you do and eat are OK, but you could look after your body better.

15 or less

Oh dear! You need to eat better food and to move your body more! Fruit and vegetables are very good for you. Eat fewer snacks and less fast food. Remember to sit down when you eat meals during the day – and don't forget that breakfast is a very important meal!

Unit wordlist

1

clothes
belt ....
coat ....
dress ....
glasses ....
glove ....
handbag ....
hat ....
jacket ....
jeans ....
pocket ....
ring ....
rucksack ....
scarf ....
shorts ....
skirt ....
sock ....
suitcase ....
tights ....
trousers ....
umbrella ....
uniform ....

body and face
back ....
finger ....
foot/feet ....
hand ....
head ....
leg ....
neck ....
nose ....

people
king ....
queen ....

places
castle ....
garden ....
wall ....

hobbies
drum ....
guitar ....
music ....

other nouns
money ....
piece of paper ....
....
story ....

verbs
carry ....
put on ....
tell someone a secret ..
....
wave ....
wear ....

adjectives
beautiful ....
blond(e) ....
clever ....
important ....
round ....
square ....

conjunctions
if ....
so ....
when ....

2

clothes
cross ....
shoe ....
spot ....
square ....
stripe ....

possessions
bag ....
newspaper ....
phone ....
towel ....

body and face
beard ....
hair ....

travel
flag ....
plane ....

animals
bear ....
bird ....
lion ....
shark ....
wing ....

the natural world
flower ....
moon ....
star ....

home
clock ....
floor ....

other nouns
drawing ....

verbs
colour ....
take off (clothes) ....
....
talk ....

adjectives
curly ....
fair ....
happy ....
long ....
sad ....
short ....
spotted ....
straight ....
striped ....
unhappy ....

3

body and face
ear ....
eye ....
mouth ....

the natural world
city ....
country ....
farm ....
farmer ....
field ....
hill ....

animals
cow ....
sheep ....
sheep dog ....

food and drink
biscuit ....
cookie ....

other nouns
telephone number ....
....

verbs
believe ....
catch (a ball) ....
....
climb ....
cook ....
cry ....
explain ....
feel ....
follow ....
forget ....
hear ....
help ....
listen ....
look ....
paint ....
point ....
remember ....
run a long way ....
....
say ....
shout ....
sing ....
smell ....
understand ....
watch ....
whisper ....
whistle ....
work very hard ....
....

adjectives

excited ....

famous ....

noisy ....

quiet ....

tired ....

the worst ....

....

prepositions

after ....

adverbs

early ....

suddenly ....

4

animals

bat ....

butterfly ....

camel ....

crocodile ....

dinosaur ....

dolphin ....

duck ....

fish ....

fly ....

fur ....

goat ....

insect ....

kangaroo ....

lizard ....

mouse ....

octopus ....

rabbit ....

spider ....

swan ....

tail ....

tiger ....

body and face

tooth/teeth ....

....

the natural world

cave ....

desert ....

forest ....

jungle ....

lake ....

plant ....

planet ....

river ....

rock ....

sea ....

water ....

places

science museum ....

....

swimming pool ....

....

zoo ....

other nouns

group ....

kind ....

part ....

adjectives

afraid of ....

dangerous ....

extinct ....

fast ....

friendly ....

adverbs

a long time ago ....

....

fast ....

quickly ....

verbs

disappear ....

fly ....

hop ....

live ....

swim ....

5

clothes

T-shirt ....

possessions

book ....

brush ....

comb ....

thing ....

torch ....

family

cousin ....

grandma ....

mother ....

mum ....

uncle ....

home

bedroom ....

mirror ....

prepositions

between ....

in front of ....

next to ....

on top of ....

verbs

brush ....

buy ....

go camping ....

....

go shopping ....

have a shower ....

hate ....

hold ....

tidy ....

use ....

adjectives

closed ....

dry ....

nice ....

open ....

tidy ....

untidy ....

6

names

first name ....

surname ....

people

best friend ....

singer ....

tennis player ....

....

school

club ....

hockey lesson ....

....

verbs

be called ....

dance ....

get off/on a train ....

....

go sailing ....

invite someone to a

party ....

....

laugh ....

meet someone ....

....

wait for a train ....

....

adjectives

excellent ....

funny ....

loud ....

same ....

thirsty ....

prepositions

before ....

opposite ....

conjunctions

before ....

expressions

Great! ....

Of course! ....

Pardon? ....

Who else? ....

Wow! ....

7

animals

parrot ....

pet ....

places

bus stop ....

corner ....

road ....

street ....

family

dad ....

parent ....

125

the natural world
beach ....
leaf/leaves ....

school
alphabet ....

time
next week ....

other nouns
dream ....
monster ....
treasure ....

verbs
agree ....
clean ....
have a meal ....
....
spell ....
steal ....

adjectives
clean ....
ready ....

prepositions
by bus ....

expressions
See you soon! ....
....
Sorry! ....

8
school
art ....
English ....
exam ....
geography ....
history ....
homework ....
language ....
maths ....
music ....
painting ....
playground ....
school day ....
science ....
sport ....
student ....

subject ....
text ....
university ....

places
library ....
town square ....

time
in the future ....
....
the past ....

verbs
bring ....
catch a bus ....
....
choose ....
find out about ....
....
learn ....
look for ....
study ....
teach ....

adjectives
all right ....
difficult ....
easy ....
good at ....

expressions
I'm not sure. ....
....

9
school
bin ....
bookcase ....
class ....
classroom ....
college ....
cupboard ....
desk ....
dictionary ....
eraser ....
glue ....
pen ....
pencil ....
rubber ....
ruler ....

scissors ....
shelf ....

verbs
complete ....
cut ....
glue ....
leave something ....
....
mean ....
tick ....
throw away ....
....

adjectives
thin ....
well ....

expressions
Anything else? ....
....
Well done! ....
....

10
colours
dark ....
light ....

the natural world
air ....
planet ....
sky ....
space ....
sun ....

travel
astronaut ....
map ....
rocket ....

sports
badminton ....
golf ....

hobbies
robot ....

other nouns
difference ....
egg ....
the end ....

verbs
look after ....
look like ....
take photos/pictures .....
....

adjectives
little ....
near ....
strange ....

adverbs
carefully ....

prepositions
until ....

11
the natural world
countryside ....
....
grass ....
island ....
mountain ....
sand ....
shell ....
waterfall ....

places
board ....
town ....
village ....

body and face
shoulder ....

clothes
sunglasses ....
sweater ....

sport and hobbies
boat ....
camera ....

food and drink
hot chocolate ....
....

other nouns
bottom ....

verbs
grow ....
ride ....

126

expressions

Good idea! ....

....

How are you? ....

....

OK! ....

What's the weather like? ....

....

What about? ....

....

What else? ....

....

12

weather

cloud ....

cold ....

fog ....

ice ....

rain ....

rainbow ....

snow ....

storm ....

temperature ....

....

wind ....

hobbies

computer games ....

....

food and drink

ice cream ....

places

park ....

slide ....

swing ....

verbs

decide ....

enjoy ....

fly a kite ....

rain ....

snow ....

stay inside ....

....

adjectives

cloudy ....

dark ....

foggy ....

hot ....

sunny ....

terrible ....

warm ....

wet ....

windy ....

worse ....

prepositions

above zero ....

....

below zero ....

....

expressions

How about..? ....

....

I know! ....

Let's... ....

Shall we ...? ....

....

13

food and drink

apple ....

banana ....

bean ....

bread ....

burger ....

butter ....

cake ....

carrot ....

cheese ....

chicken ....

chips ....

chocolate ....

coconut ....

egg ....

flour ....

fries ....

grape ....

jam ....

juice ....

lemon ....

lime ....

mango ....

meat ....

onion ....

orange ....

pasta ....

pea ....

pear ....

pineapple ....

pizza ....

potato ....

rice ....

salad ....

salt ....

sandwich ....

sausage ....

snack ....

soup ....

sugar ....

sweets ....

tomato ....

vegetable ....

watermelon ....

meals

breakfast ....

dinner ....

lunch ....

picnic ....

supper ....

home

lift ....

stairs ....

adjectives

hungry ....

sweet ....

verbs

go to bed ....

....

mix ....

move ....

adverbs

late ....

never ....

sometimes ....

....

expressions

Come on! ....

No thanks! ....

Oh dear! ....

14

animals

cage ....

elephant ....

giraffe ....

hippo ....

panda ....

whale ....

the natural world

environment ....

....

life ....

ocean ....

world ....

verbs

skip ....

15

food and drink

coffee ....

lemonade ....

milk ....

pepper ....

home

blanket ....

bottle ....

bowl ....

box ....

CD ....

chopsticks ....

cup ....

fork ....

glass ....

knife ....

plate ....

spoon ....

verbs

add salt to food ....

....

arrive ....

close your eyes ....

....

dream ....

fetch ....

pick up ....

prefer ....

127

sound (like) ....
turn off ....
turn on ....

adjectives
angry ....
bored ....
different ....
flat ....

prepositions
after ....

16
jobs
actor ....
clown ....
cook ....
doctor ....
journalist ....
mechanic ....
photographer ....
....
secretary ....
TV star ....

places
bookshop ....
café ....
restaurant ....
supermarket ....
....
theatre ....

other nouns
front page ....
news ....
problem ....

verbs
give something back .....
....
happen ....
make a film ....
....
send emails ....
....

adjectives
boring ....
busy ....

exciting ....
interesting ....

17
work
artist ....
businesswoman ....
....
engineer ....
office ....
policewoman ....
....
factory ....
meeting ....

time
a.m. ....
evening ....
half past ....
night ....
p.m. ....
quarter past/to ....
....

other nouns
conversation ....
....

verbs
begin ....
come home for lunch ...
....
finish ....
get up ....
start ....

expressions
No problem! ....
....
My watch is wrong. ......
....
What's the time? ....
....

18
work
fire engine ....
fireman ....
fire station ....
firewoman ....

police car ....
policeman ....
police station ....
....

other nouns
age ....
fire ....
traffic ....

verbs
lose ....
stop ....
telephone ....
test ....

prepositions
inside ....
outside ....

19
question words
how ....
how many ....
how much ....
how often ....
how old ....
what ....
what time ....
when ....
where ....
which ....
who ....
whose ....
why ....

food and drink
candy ....

family
aunt ....
brother ....
father ....
grandpa ....
sister ....

verbs
end ....
shop ....
ski ....

adjectives
expensive ....

adverbs
ever ....
once ....

expressions
All right! ....
Yes, please! ....
....

20
people
baby ....
grown-up ....

places
London ....

home
chair ....
stamp ....

adjectives
awake ....
empty ....
full ....

adverbs
always ....
yet ....

verbs
fall over ....
get wet ....
make friends ....
....
send a letter ....
....
smile ....

expressions
That sounds interesting!
....

21
body and face
arm ....
stomach ....

health

ambulance ....

ambulance driver ....

....

chemist's ....

cold ....

cough ....

dentist ....

earache ....

headache ....

hospital ....

medicine ....

nurse ....

stomach-ache ....

....

toothache ....

....

home

soap ....

adjectives

better ....

broken ....

fine ....

ill ....

verbs

have a temperature ......

....

hurt ....

lie down ....

expressions

Poor boy! ....

What's the matter? ....

....

Why don't you...? ....

....

Thank you ....

22

time

autumn ....

century ....

date ....

fall ....

hour ....

midday ....

midnight ....

minute ....

month ....

spring ....

summer ....

today ....

tomorrow ....

tonight ....

weekend ....

winter ....

year ....

yesterday ....

months

January ....

February ....

March ....

April ....

May ....

June ....

July ....

August ....

September ....

October ....

November ....

December ....

sports and hobbies

camping ....

diary ....

sandcastle ....

skiing ....

wish ....

verbs

fall ....

taste ....

determiners

each ....

every ....

expressions

make a snowman ....

....

throw snowballs ....

....

23

numbers

hundred ....

kilometre ....

thousand ....

sport

golf ball ....

golfer ....

family

husband ....

wife ....

other nouns

birthday party ....

....

birthday present ....

cinema ....

movie ....

ticket ....

adjectives

far ....

high ....

tall ....

adverbs

already ....

also ....

only ....

verbs

film ....

hit ....

pass a test ....

24

travel

airport ....

bicycle ....

driver ....

helicopter ....

lorry ....

motorbike ....

plane ....

taxi ....

truck ....

verbs

drop ....

get to a place ....

....

go for a ride ....

....

go somewhere on foot

....

have problems ....

....

adjectives

quick ....

slow ....

prepositions

without ....

25

body and face

face ....

possessions

flashlight ....

paintbrush ....

....

toothbrush ....

....

verbs

clean your teeth ....

....

go away ....

go on holiday ....

....

have a wash ....

....

have a snack ....

....

wash your hands ....

....

adjectives

brave ....

dirty ....

furry ....

naughty ....

surprised ....

ugly ....

expressions

I don't mind. ....

....

Right! ....

26

home

apartment ....

garage ....

the first floor ....

....

places
hotel ....

station ....

verbs
be away from home .....

....

get ready ....

go climbing ....

need ....

sleep in a tent ....

....

stay in a hotel ....

....

visit ....

adjectives
last ....

27
people
pirate ....

other nouns
piece of wood ....

....

sea monster ....

....

verbs
hide ....

actions
bounce a ball ....

....

comb your hair ....

....

do your homework ......

....

email a friend ....

....

finish school ....

....

get undressed ....

....

go to sleep ....

....

jump into bed ....

....

kick a ball ....

....

leave home ....

....

make a wish ....

....

speak to your friends ...

....

study English ....

....

wave goodbye ....

....

expressions
It's time to go ....

....

What a great place! ....

....

28
sports and hobbies
football club ....

....

team ....

work
footballer ....

postman ....

ticket office ....

verbs
get into a car ....

....

get out of a car ....

....

score ....

thank someone ....

....

win ....

29
materials
glass ....

gold ....

metal ....

paper ....

plastic ....

wood ....

wool ....

home
card ....

envelope ....

fan ....

key ....

toy ....

verbs
be made of ....

....

adjectives
hard ....

prepositions
through ....

30
home
cooker ....

fridge ....

kitchen ....

magazine ....

note ....

scissors ....

colours and materials
gold ....

silver ....

prepositional phrases
on the left ....

....

on the right ....

....

31
places
bus station ....

....

clothes shop ....

....

post office ....

sports centre ....

....

sports shop ....

store ....

sweet shop ....

verbs
sell ....

adjectives
cheap ....

horrible ....

lovely ....

kind ....

soft ....

32
places
circus ....

post box ....

pyramid ....

work
pilot ....

verbs
have time to ....

....

pay ....

post a letter ....

....

show ....

adjectives
unfriendly ....

adverbs
here ....

over there ....

expressions
Excuse me? ....

Follow me please! ....

Here you are! ....

....

How can I help? ....

....

33
clothes
light clothes ....

....

walking shoes ....

....

warm clothes ....

....

130

places
market ....
sports club ....
....

sports and hobbies
programme ....
....
skate ....
skis ....
ski school ....
sledge ....
snow sports ....
....
the news ....

verbs
go up in a lift ....
....
take a taxi ....
....

conjunctions
because ....

34
animals
cat ....
frog ....
horse ....
monkey ....
snake ....

people
grandparent ....
....

food and drink
lunch box ....

sports and hobbies
competition ....
....
DVD ....
sound ....

verbs
guess ....
put up a tent ....
....
swing ....
wake someone ....
....

wake up ....
....
wish ....

determiners
both ....

expressions
I have no idea! ....
....

35
sports and hobbies
baseball ....
basketball ....
dancing ....
fishing ....
player ....
race ....
skating ....
soccer ....
table tennis ....
....
volleyball ....

home
ground ....

verbs
fish ....
pull ....
push ....
skate ....
try ....

prepositions
across ....

36
family
grandfather ....
....
grandmother ....
....

animals
puppy ....

clothes
shirt ....
swimming shorts ....
....

the natural world
the light of the moon ...
....
....

verbs
count ....
sail a ship ....

adverbs
often ....
usually ....

prepositions
behind ....
under ....

37
sports and hobbies
comic ....

school
schoolwork ....
....

time
afternoon ....
Christmas ....
Monday ....
morning ....
Saturday ....
Sunday ....

verbs
plant ....

adverbs
at first ....
still ....

38
food and drink
tea ....

other nouns
postcard ....

verbs
spend money ....

expressions
Dear Nick, ...
It was fine. ....

Lots of love from
(Mary) ....
....

39
sports and hobbies
ski lift ....
skier ....
snowboarding ....
....

places
New York ....

determiners
all of ....
a few of ....
half of ....
most of ....
some of ....

pronouns
everyone ....
no-one ....

40
home
armchair ....
basement ....
radio ....
window ....

other nouns
invitation ....

verbs
call (a puppy/a baby) ...
....
have a party ....
....
miss the bus ....
....

adverbs
just ....

expressions
Which one? ....
Later perhaps! ....
....

131

He's always late for .....

....

Nothing else for me. .....

....

41

home
balcony ....
bath ....
bathroom ....
CD player ....
dining room ....

....

elevator ....
flat ....
front door ....
hall ....
lamp ....
light ....
living room ....

....

mat ....
picture ....
sofa ....
table ....
tape recorder ....

....

toilet ....
video ....

animals
kitten ....

body and face
moustache ....

verbs
get dark ....
move to a house ....

....

adjectives
correct ....

adverbs
downstairs ....
upstairs ....

expressions
Wait a minute ....

....

42

time
five o'clock ....
Friday ....
leap year ....
Thursday ....
Tuesday ....
Wednesday ....

....

verbs
change ....

adjectives
right ....

43

verbs
may ....
might ....
will ....
won't ....

adjectives
married ....
single ....

44

daily life
address ....
free time ....

family
children ....
daughter ....
granddaughter ....

....

grandson ....
son ....

names
Miss ....
Mr ....
Mrs ....

hobbies
horse-riding ....

....

water-skiing ....

....

travel
sports car ....

....

verbs
go for a walk ....

....

adjectives
double ....

expressions
Bye for now! ....

If you don't mind. ....

Let me think. ....

....

45

work
animal doctor ....

....

business ....
dolphin trainer ....

....

film star ....
golf player ....
horse rider ....
train driver ....

other nouns
film studio ....
music group ....

....

verbs
go for a run ....

....

phone ....

46

places
car factory ....
computer room ....

....

sports hall ....

computers
home page ....
website ....

sports
line ....
ski teacher ....
ski team ....

other nouns
coconut tree ....

....

library card ....

....

verbs
burn ....

prepositions
down ....
since ....
up ....

47

places
bridge ....

adjectives
missing ....
poor ....
rich ....

adverbs
somewhere ....

....

48

language
capital letter ....

....

full stop ....
question mark ....

sentence ....
word ....

adjectives
old ....
strong ....
weak ....
young ....

verbs
go out ....

....

132

adverbs
anywhere ....
enough ....
too ....

49
verbs
practise ....
run in a race ....
....

adverbs
together ....

50
school
spelling ....

verbs
do an exam/a test ....
....
do some shopping ....
....
do sport ....
....
do work ....
....
do homework ....
....
have fun ....
....
make a mistake ....
....
make a bed ....
....
make a pizza ....
....

adjectives
fun ....

51
school
language school ....
....

hobbies
piano ....

pop music ....

question words
how long ....

52
hobbies
board game ....
....
doll ....

adverbs
quietly ....

pronouns
anyone ....

53
travel
east ....
north ....
south ....
west ....

hobbies
go fishing ....
have a lesson ....
....
learn to sail ....
....
learn to water-ski ....
....
water-skiing classes ......
....

other nouns
length ....

adverbs
everywhere ....
nowhere ....

determiners
another ....
other ....

pronouns
everything ....

expressions
go on a boat ride ....
....
go to work ....
....

54
places
bank ....
side ....

travel
cross the street ....
....
go past ....
go straight on ....
....
turn left ....
turn right ....

other nouns
the Internet ....
....

verbs
take a long time ....
....

expressions
Can I help you? ....
....
How do I get to..? ....
....
What a beautiful day! ..
....
What's the quickest way
to..? ....
....

55
work
waiter ....

hobbies
word game ....
....

verbs
cross out ....

133

Irregular verbs

Verb	Past simple	Past participle	Translation
be	was/were	been	....
begin	began	begun	....
break	broke	broken	....
bring	brought	brought	....
burn	burnt	burnt	....
buy	bought	bought	....
can	could	–	....
catch	caught	caught	....
choose	chose	chosen	....
come	came	come	....
cut	cut	cut	....
do	did	done	....
draw	drew	drawn	....
dream	dreamed/dreamt	dreamed/dreamt	....
drink	drank	drunk	....
drive	drove	driven	....
eat	ate	eaten	....
fall	fell	fallen	....
feel (like)	felt	felt	....
find	found	found	....
fly	flew	flown	....
forget	forgot	forgotten	....
get	got	got	....
get up	got up	got up	....
give	gave	given	....
go	went	gone	....
grow	grew	grown	....
have	had	had	....
have to	had to	had to	....
hear	heard	heard	....
hide	hid	hidden	....
hit	hit	hit	....
hold	held	held	....
hurt	hurt	hurt	....
know	knew	known	....
learn	learned/learnt	learned/learnt	....
leave	left	left	....
let	let	let	....
lie down	lay down	lain down	....

Verb	Past simple	Past participle	Translation
lose	lost	lost	....
make	made	made	....
mean	meant	meant	....
meet	met	met	....
put	put	put	....
read	read	read	....
ride	rode	ridden	....
run	ran	run	....
say	say	said	....
see	saw	seen	....
sell	sold	sold	....
send	sent	sent	....
sing	sang	sung	....
sit (down)	sat	sat	....
sleep	slept	slept	....
smell	smelled/smelt	smelled/smelt	....
speak	spoke	spoken	....
spell	spelled/spelt	spelled/spelt	....
spend	spent	spent	....
stand (up)	stood	stood	....
steal	stole	stolen	....
swim	swam	swum	....
swing	swung	swung	....
take	took	taken	....
take off	took off	taken off	....
teach	taught	taught	....
tell	told	told	....
think	thought	thought	....
throw	threw	thrown	....
understand	understood	understood	....
wake up	woke up	woken up	....
wear	wore	worn	....
win	won	won	....
write	wrote	written	....